Praise for Finding Roses in the Dust

Trusting God is a great theory – and wonderful theology. But to actually do it is another thing – particularly when that trust calls you to say "yes" to a faith journey that most people in America would think is crazy. Through Erin Brynn's eyes I have seen a part of the world through God's eyes. Through her engaging writing, I have seen the history, culture, and people of Afghanistan differently. Who would think of a calling to Kabul as a "gift from God"? Only an adventurous Christ-follower! Read this and be challenged to be more deeply involved in what God is doing in the world.

Jay Barnes, PhD
President
Bethel University

D1372809

Erin emphasizes the importance of seeing our world through God's lenses. In my experience, everything depends on the way we see our world. She writes *"we all carry blinders that are so tall and so wide. If we are willing to hear God's voice and follow Him, He will take off our blinders."*

This book is a challenge that will take you out of your comfort zone. John 4:35 says, *"Don't say there is still four months and then comes the harvest; lift up your eyes, look at the fields, for they are already white for harvest."* That is what our Father sees.

Erin will challenge you in this book to see what our Father sees and what our part is to be. What an extraordinary tale, an adventure, a walk of obedience in the perfect will of God. Are you willing to open your eyes and see?

Terry Law
Founder and President of World Compassion

Responding to devastating disasters worldwide has linked my life with the Brynn's in the crucible of shared experiences while meeting the needs of desperate, hurting people. I was deeply impacted by this book as I saw Afghanistan through Erin's eyes and followed the profound changes that worked in her life as God revealed His love for the Afghan people. After reading her book, I will never "see" Afghanistan the same. I, too, have come to see the Roses in the dust through the eyes of a courageous woman who saw Afghanistan through the eyes of Jesus.

Paul R. Williams, MD
President, International HealthCare Network

Although the book focuses on life in Afghanistan, it is really about God's transformation in Erin. Amazing! She made me cry and laugh out loud, sometimes at the same time, and, of course, I shouted "amen" a few times as well!

Karen, former teacher in Afghanistan

Perhaps the last place you thought you would want to visit is Afghanistan. This book will take you there, and you will be glad you went! Through the eyes of a mom and wife, you will take off your blinders and learn to love its people. I'm glad I made the trip!

David Stevens, MD, M.A. (Ethics) CEO, CMDA

This book is inspirational, heart-warming, educational, and captivating. I felt I was taken on a journey and a whole new world was opened to me. Thank you for being willing servants of Jesus Christ and for showing me how God uses ordinary people to do the extraordinary. It touches my heart to see how much God loves those who are lost and the tremendous lengths He goes to share His love and goodness with them.

Wendy, from Missouri

We've never had such a clash of religions or cultures in our world as we are having now. I pray this reaches far and wide and finds the hearts of those who need it most!! Erin is so gifted in her expression and I appreciate her vulnerability with just being real in her experiences. Thank you for going, for sharing, and for planting HUGE spiritual gardens.

Heidi, from Oklahoma

What a timely, accurate view into the heart of God for the people of Afghanistan! Erin's perspective is a Spirit-call to each of us to believe and intercede for healing and redemption where brokenness and turmoil have had their way. A must read!

Pastor Ron Woods, Oklahoma

This book is more informative and entertaining than many books about missions that I have read. Erin is honest and transparent, humble, bold, humorous, vulnerable, and compassionate. I can relate to her. She behaves and speaks like an ordinary human being who is relying on the grace of God on a daily basis. Her stories smack of real life. Erin shares her joys and successes as well as her pain.

Cheyn Onarecker, MD
St. Anthony Family Medicine

I have partnered with and admired this family for years. Having been to Afghanistan myself, I must admit I thought they were a bit crazy to move there. However, God always equips us for what He calls us to do. This book is an excellent look inside a culture that most have only formed their opinions of from CNN. I have learned over the years that that is a very narrow approach. To truly understand another man's culture, you must walk alongside him. That is what this family did, and this book reflects that journey very well.

David L. Meyer
CEO, Hand of Hope

It is a pleasure to endorse this superb account of one woman's pilgrimage of spiritual growth while in Afghanistan. It is an inspirational, powerful, personal look deep within herself as well as at the Afghan people, which led to a period of loving service in that country. Her colorful personal stories of adjustment and the people are riveting and relate to all people in all cultures.

Warren Heffron, MD
Department of Family & Community Medicine,
University of New Mexico

Finding Roses in the Dust

A Journey to a New Perspective

Erin Brynn

WestBow
P R E S S
A DIVISION OF THOMAS NELSON

WestBow Press books may be ordered through booksellers or by contacting:

WestBow Press
A Division of Thomas Nelson
1663 Liberty Drive
Bloomington, IN 47403
www.westbowpress.com
1-(866) 928-1240

ISBN: 978-1-4497-9507-8 (sc)
ISBN: 978-1-4497-9508-5 (hc)
ISBN: 978-1-4497-9506-1 (e)

Library of Congress Control Number: 2013908732

Printed in the United States of America.

WestBow Press rev. date: 6/7/2013

Dedication

The dedication of this book is three-fold: first, to my husband William, my prince, for without his obedience and example there would be no journeys and no stories to tell. You, my love, are the backbone of this project; without you, I would have abandoned this all long ago. Thank you for pushing me to be more than I thought I could be. Thank you for the hours and hours of work editing, reading, making phone calls and filtering all the details so I could write. You, my love, are my gift from the Lord, my perfect partner, my inspiration and my compass, always pointing me towards truth. Thank you! I love you with all my heart.

Second, to my precious friends Joe and Kate who have sacrificed so much for the people of Afghanistan. You, my friends, have taught me how to open my heart in ways I didn't think were possible. Your constant desire to do God's will while living out the authentic love of Christ before all Afghans has stretched and touched me. What you do every day at the cost of family, comfort, and wealth is an inspiration to me and many others. Thank you for accepting the "Call" to go and for being willing to love this crazy family that you let move into your world.

Third, to the expatriate community of Afghanistan. To the men and women who have given their all to help the Afghan people know the "Truth." Some have come for weeks, others for years; but all share the desire and compelling urge to reveal Jesus to a lost world. Thank you for what you have all given up to live a crazy, wonderful, amazing and sometimes scary Afghan life. And to those foreigners who have paid the ultimate sacrifice for Afghanistan…their lives - martyrs for the call. Your lives have inspired and pushed us toward the mark. "Well done, good and faithful servants!"

I lift up my eyes to the hills-where does my help come from? My help comes from the Lord, the Maker of heaven and earth.

- King David

TABLE of CONTENTS

PART THREE
Lessons from the Journey

ACKNOWLEDGMENTS

Thank You, Lord, for revealing Yourself to me, for making me Your child. Thank You for giving me this most amazing, crazy, challenging, wonderful life. Thank You for giving me a glimpse of Your heart for the world and for patiently molding and shaping me into a tool that can be used for Your purposes. Most of all, thank You for showing me how very much You love me.

Thank you, William, my "Indiana Jones," my "prince" who rescued me from a boring, mundane life. I am so grateful that you chose me to be your partner in this world. Your stability and wisdom have navigated our family through the craziest of storms. You are a general in God's army. Your steadfast strength and loyalty to the call on our family has been the compass that has directed us always to Christ. Thank you, Honey, for loving me with an unconditional love that, next to Jesus, no one in this world has done! Most of all, thank you for loving Jesus more than any earthly thing!

Thank you, Emma, Alex, Joy, Mitchell, Hank, and Laney, my amazing children; you are the most precious gifts that God has given me in this life. The scripture in Psalm 127:3 says that you are my reward; God really loves me! You challenge me every day to be a better mom and woman. Watching your love and obedience to Christ has been one of life's greatest treasures. Thank you for putting up with this project, for understanding the tears that it has brought and the preciousness of its gifts. Thank you for the sacrifices you have made for the people of Afghanistan. I love you all so very much!

Thank you to my editors. Linda, thank you for believing in this project sometimes even more than I. Thank you for seeing and respecting the vision I had for this story; and, most of all, thank you for putting all things to prayer seeking God through every step of the process. Your life and convictions have been an inspiration to me and your friendship a sweet blessing. DeLayne, thank you for partnering with me while navigating through your own very full life. Thank you for sharing your gift of detail with this project, seeing all the "little" things so often missed. Your work ethic and focus on the small things has pushed and challenged me to be more. You have been a precious gift to this project. Dr. Mark, your ideas, suggestions, and edits were vital in helping bring this project to the finish line!

Thank you to the host of people who have encouraged us and prayed for us through this journey. Linda and Heidi, your prayers and words in season got me through many a day. My precious sister Joy, your shoulder to cry on and hearing you say "I understand" brought grounding to me over and over. Thank you to both moms and dads; wow! Your amazing support has been such a foundation to our lives. You have believed God for us even when it seemed crazy to do so. Thank you for trusting us, for trusting the call in us, and for letting your grandchildren go to foreign and sometimes unsafe places. Thank you for the hours of prayer given to us and the people we have loved. Thank you for giving so we could go.

Thank you to all the precious people who partnered with us so we could make this trip to Afghanistan. Thank you for believing in what God is doing in that country. Thank you for giving and praying and for seeing God's heart in this endeavor. Your reward will be great!

Joe and Amy, thank you for running our lives in our absence so many times, for loving our children and believing in the things that God has called us to do. Your support has made many trips possible for us; we love and appreciate you so very much!

Thank you, Jim and Barb, for convincing me to tell this story. Without your encouragement and help, there would never have been one word put to paper.

Thank you, Joe and Kate, for being our "home away from home"—for loving us, laughing with us, crying with us, and for showing us what the family of God is all about. It is truly an honor to stand beside you in the army of God!

Thank you, Steffan Carriger, for your creative input, for giving a name to the nameless. Your heart and passion challenge and bless me.

Thank you to all my faithful "letter" readers. Thank you for giving me an audience to share the stories of this misunderstood place and details of what was going on in my own heart. Thank you for your words of encouragement and prayers of faith. Without you, I would have had no one to whom I could tell my stories.

PROLOGUE

The pages that follow are the written record of a journey given to me as a gift from my heavenly Father. This journey helped me to discover a new perspective of His world and His people. This was a journey of love, hope, fear, frustration, and ultimately freedom that changed who I am and the way I look at life.

These letters chronicle a year of my life living in Afghanistan, a country filled with war, evil, beauty, revelation, and friendships. God, through the everyday, broke the lenses of my perspective and replaced them with a clarity of vision that I believe is closer to the vision of the Father than I could have achieved on my own.

My prayer is that as you take this journey with me, you will allow God to redirect your focus to what He sees and enable you to perceive and love the way He does.

Afghanistan is a country that has been torn apart and broken by war for generations. In the spring and early summer, beautiful wild roses miraculously appear out of the dust of the land. Some roses defiantly emerge from garbage heaps while others quietly appear in corners completely unnoticed by those passing by. The roses fill the land with bright spots of color and beauty where usually there is only dirt and broken debris. The roses remind the people of Afghanistan what their country was like before it was destroyed by bullets and rockets. They remind me of the beauty of the people of this harsh place and the love that our Father has for them. The roses also remind me that no matter where I lay my head at night, regardless of how hopeless and difficult my surroundings may seem, there are always beautiful roses waiting to push through the dirt of my life. God desires to feed, cultivate, and weed the garden of my heart so that the most beautiful and vibrantly colored flowers can bloom and turn their faces toward the "Son." They reminded me to daily look for the beauty amid the brokenness, for there is always beauty if we look hard enough. The roses of Afghanistan appear each spring like kisses from God, a reminder that God loves His children and desires for them to know Him. Afghanistan is a broken land with many broken people; but it is also a land filled with people created in God's image, people who have been deceived, broken, feared, and forgotten. My hope is that this story will reveal the authentic beauty of God's bouquet of these people and will inspire you to love and pray for them, believing in faith for their blooms to open and turn toward the "Son."

PART ONE

Preparing for the Journey

CHAPTER 1 – An Unexpected Gift

Matthew 14:14

And when Jesus went out He saw a great multitude; and He was moved with compassion for them, and healed their sick.

There are very few times in life that something happens that is so dramatic that it changes the way we see the world. When it does happen, it changes our perspective in such a way that everything seems different and new. Life seems to suddenly make sense, and we begin to know our purpose. When the pieces fall together so that our perspective changes, it's miraculous. To see a person or situation so radically different than before changes the core of who we are; to take the blinders off our vision and see the width and depth of the world around us, to metamorphose from one person and way of thinking to another is a rare and often painful experience. When we are allowed to feel and experience life through another's eyes and then struggle through the beliefs that we thought were right but may indeed be wrong, it can be a gift of priceless proportion. The process may not always be easy or lovely or make us comfortable, but it is a gift nonetheless. The magnitude of that gift can only be measured on the other side of the journey as we look back and see that we are no longer the person we thought we were; we are more; we are better. Anytime we are allowed to step outside of ourselves, to know and understand another's world or be given a glimpse of what our Father God sees without the filter of our selfishness, we cannot help but be radically changed. Our hearts become bigger and fuller, and our capacity to love and be loved becomes greater and greater.

One day in late spring, as life was swirling with all its activities—six children and a busy medical practice—my husband and I were presented with just such a gift. We were asked to consider moving to Kabul, Afghanistan. Of course, at the time we made the decision to go, I had no idea my perspective needed to change or what a gift it would be. I also had no idea how painful and ugly the process would end up being. I have spent my entire adult life being involved in traveling and ministry in other countries in the world. I saw myself as a fairly well rounded, open-minded person.

4

I have lived in Africa and have traveled to and experienced many different cultures over the past 25 years. I thought my perspective was rather broad and diverse. I didn't know that I carried with me blinders so tall and so wide that it was impossible to have the understanding and clarity I thought I had. I had no idea that my heart held judgment and prejudice so deep and ugly that I would end up being ashamed and broken. The blinders of my perspective had limited my view and kept me from seeing the world through God's eyes.

If we are hindered from viewing life through the lens of God's eye, then we are destined, no matter how hard we try, to live a life filtered by selfishness and pride. By removing the blinders, our perspective is altered. We go from a narrow, limited view of the world to limitless opportunities for knowledge and growth. Sometimes taking the blinders off can be painful, sad, and overwhelming. The confusion and sense of responsibility that comes from seeing others suffer can be devastating. So if we place blinders on and focus only on what lies directly in our paths, we can go through life "feeling" happier and better about ourselves and others.

Though we may think it is easier, life with blinders is not the life that God intends us to live. God intends us to have the same view He has. He wants us to see and experience His world—its beauty and its brokenness, and His people—their joys and their sufferings. If we cannot see what God sees, how can we do His work? How can we obey Him? How can we love others as ourselves as we are instructed in Mathew 19:19? Is it possible to "live a Christian life" and only be focused on ourselves? How can brokenness and suffering be helped and ministered to if we, the hands and feet of Jesus, are not willing to even admit that it exists?

Moving to Afghanistan forced me to take off some blinders that I was not even aware I had. My home, my children, my friends, and family were no longer right in front of me keeping my attention from straying too far to the left or right. Suddenly

I was painfully aware that I needed to see life and the people of Afghanistan the way that God sees them. Left to my own perspective, I was doomed to lead a lonely, fearful life. God doesn't see people through a lens of politics, war, poverty, or lack. God sees all people as His creation, people who are separated from Him. He made each and every child with a plan and purpose and an internal emptiness that can only be filled with Him. God's heart grieves for these children; His heart is broken for the suffering and violence they experience. For me, understanding God's heart toward the people of Afghanistan would be the foundation of a new perspective. That new perspective would usher in a new revelation, not only of the life around me, but for His love toward me.

CHAPTER 2 – Eleven Simple Words

1 Samuel 15:22

Behold, to obey is better than sacrifice,
and to heed than the fat of rams.

When I first allowed myself to even entertain the thought of moving to a war zone and terrorist-filled country, I felt utter panic. I argued and wrestled with God, explaining that this could not possibly be the time He would choose to ask us to relocate our family. We had just graduated our oldest child from college, another was starting his senior year in college, and another was beginning her sophomore year. Our fourth was graduating from high school, and the two younger ones were in junior high, ages 11 and 13. I couldn't help but think how absolutely irresponsible it would be for us to consider leaving four of our kids behind while we tromped off to some volatile place halfway around the world. What about our house, my husband's practice, and our many responsibilities? What about the reactions of our families and friends? I thought there was no way our parents would be supportive of us moving their precious grandchildren to a country at war. The questions were endless, and there seemed to be no answers. As the weeks went by, both my husband and I were wrestling with the invitation. One day while we were driving, I finally got the nerve to ask my husband out loud, "So, what about Afghanistan?" There was a part of me that couldn't believe I had just spoken those words and another part that took a huge sigh of relief. The pregnant pause that hung in the air stopped time for me, and then I heard my husband answer with what I knew he would say all along, "I think we should go." And so the journey began.

As I pondered the words my husband had just spoken, I began to cry. I cried with the realization that my biggest fear was coming to pass, and I had no idea what to do with it. I grew up in church believing God has called every one of us to "the world." I have had no problem believing God for protection, provision, and grace for short-term trips or even for the two years we spent living in Africa with our family. However, this was different. God was asking us to leave some of our children, our home, our extended family, and our busy lives to go into a dangerous country to help people considered to be our enemies. I knew in my heart that God loved the people of Afghanistan, and I also knew He wanted us to help them. I had visited Afghanistan five years earlier and had seen the pain and desperation in the eyes of the people. I knew most were not our enemies; they were war-weary lost lives crying out for help. However, visiting there and moving there to live were two different things.

When I visited Kabul five years earlier, it was both shocking and familiar. Most developing countries have distinct similarities: open gutters where sewer and trash flow, broken down buildings, and structures started but never finished; chickens, sheep, and cows openly grazing in the streets; heaps of trash on every corner and unorganized traffic with many people seemingly going nowhere; and the smell of baking bread and diesel hanging in the air. Somehow the chaos must make sense to someone. However, in Kabul, people not only live with poverty and lack and chaos, they must also contend with the weight of fear and oppression much greater than I have ever seen. The years of war and terror have changed the city from a cultural Mecca to a hollow shell, housing over four million empty-eyed people—people who no longer trust their neighbors or even their closest family members; people who will sell their own children for food or money to feed their opium addictions; people who risk their lives every day simply by going to work or crossing the city—people silently screaming for help, help to find peace; not only for physical peace, but for heart peace.

As I sat in the open silence of the car that day pondering my previous experience in this forgotten land, I felt panicked, overwhelmed, incompetent, and anything but able to accept what was before me. It reminded me of the time when Jesus saw the multitudes.

> *When He saw the throngs, He was moved with pity*
> *and sympathy for them because they were bewildered*

> *like sheep without a shepherd. Then He said to His dis-*
> *ciples, "The harvest is indeed plentiful, but the labor-*
> *ers are few. So pray to the Lord of the harvest to force*
> *out and thrust laborers into His harvest. (Amplified*
> *Version)"* (Matthew 9:35-38)

This is what we are supposed to do. We get very busy with houses and lives and cars and jobs and schools and families and all the things that are really important. But the bottom line is that the reason we are here is to participate with God in reaching the nations, in reaching people, in extending His kingdom to those who don't know. Whether it is locally, in our nation, or around the world, we are to pray to the Lord of the harvest for laborers to be sent to the fields. I knew in my heart God was asking us to go to Afghanistan and become laborers for Him.

For the next several days I walked around in a daze, my mind constantly swirling with the *"what if's"* and *"How can we's?"* The possibility of relocating would mean a tremendous adjustment and heavy load for those in our personal as well as professional lives. Many things would need to fall into place, so we kept the life-altering decision to ourselves with the exception of sharing with several close friends we knew would pray and seek the Lord with us.

The turning point came for me one morning as I was preparing for the day. I was having a pity party with the Lord, complaining to Him about all the difficult things He seemed to be requiring of me. Like Moses, I explained to Him how I really didn't think I was qualified to do what He was asking me to do. I kept challenging Him, "But what about this? What about that?" Inwardly I was kicking my feet and shouting, "Why do I have to do this?" Suddenly, the Spirit of God just settled on me, and I heard the Lord's voice, not audibly, but no doubt His voice inside me, answering, *"You don't HAVE to do this...* *You GET to do this!"* In that very moment, God broke my heart for the people of Afghanistan. With eleven simple words from God, everything changed for me. In a split second, I went from feeling like I would be overtaken with panic, fear, and dread to not being able to get my suitcases packed fast enough! God was changing my perspective. God was helping me to see things the way He does. In that moment, I didn't care about the list of questions I had and all of the details involved in preparing to leave. I no longer cared about all the reasons we couldn't possibly do something like this. Now I only cared about all the reasons we *had to.* I was thinking of how ridiculous it would be *not* to follow God to Afghanistan and how selfish it would be to deprive my children of experiencing this journey along with us. God was asking us to partner with Him in His plan to touch the world.

As I stood weeping, this time with gratitude and joy, I realized what an amazing privilege it is to serve God, to obey Him, and to walk out the plans and purposes He has for our lives. Going to Afghanistan would be a gift of immeasurable wealth. It would be an opportunity for our family to live out what we truly believe, to live for the One in Whom we believe. And it would be an opportunity to live and work in one of the most powerful ways with the people of this land, through servant leadership. Perhaps by daily working hand in hand, being in relationship with them, and living life together, there might be an opportunity to present truth and hope to the people of this broken country.

A Partnership Built on Faith

The revelation of our partnership with God came full circle for me one early August afternoon as William and I were sitting in an interview with the organization that would be helping us get settled in Afghanistan. In the middle of our meeting, the director conducting the interview received a phone call. I could tell by the way he was speaking that something was terribly wrong. After several minutes, he explained to us what he had just learned: ten foreign men and women working on a medical outreach had been shot and killed in northern Afghanistan. The team had been murdered in broad daylight as they traveled from a clinic sight in Nuristan back to Kabul. These men and women were people just like us, people wanting to help the poor and needy of this country. Most of the team members were doctors and nurses who had committed to traveling several days by car to a northern area of Afghanistan and then hiking up the mountains to provide a medical and eye clinic for people living in that remote location. Some of the team members had lived in Afghanistan for more than 25 years, spoke the language, and considered Afghanistan "home." My husband had actually met some of the members during a prior visit to Kabul. These deaths were an enormous loss on many levels.

While William and I listened to the details of this phone call, it became very clear to me that moving to Afghanistan posed a real threat. Our family could have been on that very team! Would I be willing to risk my life for what God was asking us to do? At that very moment, I knew this tragic news would not change my mind about going. If anything, it only inspired a greater resolve in us that we must go! The timing was perfect, and we would not allow fear to dictate our actions. However, I would be lying if I told you I didn't struggle at times with the news of the deaths of these precious people; the team had paid the ultimate sacrifice for Afghanistan—their lives.

The Grace to Say Yes

As the details of what happened unfolded, I knew that within 24 hours the world would learn of this horrific tragedy. There would be a risk of the borders closing and the possibility our visas would not be approved. There were also many well-meaning friends who would write or call us and say, "Surely you will not be going now." It took an act of our will to walk in faith and not fear as we continued making plans to leave. I had to learn to trust God to protect all of us, both here in America and abroad. And perhaps most importantly, I had to ask myself the question, "What if?" What would I choose to believe, and where would I put my trust if confronted with death? Was I ready to die? Could I completely trust God to care for my family? Could I trust God completely with my life and all the details of it? These are questions I will always struggle with as I walk the road of life. However, for this particular time and situation, I had the grace to say, "Yes." God allowed me to see the situation through His eyes; His perspective became mine! As we partnered with God, I knew that no matter what happened, I would commit to hearing His voice and following His lead and trusting Him for protection, provision, wisdom, and grace.

The weeks following our decision to go were a blur as we sorted through details, questions and timing. Knowing with certainty that we were supposed to make this move gave us peace that the Lord would work out all of the unknowns. Most people plan for upwards of a year for a major move like this. At the time of our decision, we had about ten weeks; and when we made our decision public, we were just six weeks from our departure.

After making the decision to go to Afghanistan, the first order of business for us was to tell our children. Four of them would be staying behind, and two of them would be going with us, and all would be directly affected by the changes our family was making.

It was difficult to know what the best timing was for revealing our news; the older children who would be staying behind would be the least affected, so we decided to tell them first. Though primarily it would be William's and my decision about going, we did desire the children's input and wanted to make sure they felt included in the details. They needed to know their opinion was valued and that if the decision for us to move to a war torn country was right for half of us, it was right for all eight of us. We decided to hold off on telling Laney and Hank because the adjustment would be the biggest for them. Thinking about leaving their friends and school and sports teams for two months before departure seemed like it would be torture for them, so we waited until just a few weeks before we left to tell them. Both meetings went well but were full of emotion.

When we told the older kids, they were worried mostly about what to do if they needed money or if their computers broke or what they would do when school was on break. Our oldest, Emma, would be taking care of our house and dogs and bills, and the youngest of the four, Mitchell, would be going off to his freshman year at college. Joy and Alex would be finishing their sophomore and senior years at college, so life would stay basically the same for them, at least during the school months. After lots of discussions and question-answering, the bottom line for all of them was that if this was what God was asking us to do, then, of course, we needed to go, and they would all be fine and do what they needed to do to take care of each other and all the details of their lives while we were gone.

Telling Laney and Hank was quite a bit more emotional and difficult. They didn't want to leave their friends, their school, and their "world" of security and predictability. As I look back on it, how could a 12- and 13-year-old possibly understand their parents ripping them out of the only life they knew to go live in a place they have only heard about as dangerous and one to be feared? The amount of trust and resolve they both showed during this transition was amazing. Later, after being in Afghanistan for a few months, Hank told us that he loved our little house and life and was so glad that we were not living in a tent in the mountains. He had thought for all those weeks leading up to moving that we would be living in a tent the entire time. Though he feared what it would be like and wondered if he could do it, he never once said a word to us, but instead trusted us to take care of him. When we landed in Afghanistan and rode in the van that would take us to our new home, Hank and Laney were wide-eyed with wonder, watching the traffic and people and sights of their new country. At one point Hank leaned over to her and said, "Laney, this is going to be the best adventure of our lives." To this day, Hank will say that statement is still true. Hank especially misses our life there and often asks if he can go back.

The day we told the younger two about our decision was a day filled with tears and fear and sadness for them. In the days and months to come, God was mindful of our children. He took amazing care of them and not only provided a beautiful place for them to live and grow but gave them meaningful relationships and treasured gifts of culture and experiences that will go with them to help shape their perspectives for the rest of their lives. Everything they received was above and beyond what they had thought or expected. Our time in Afghanistan as a "small" family gave Laney and Hank concentrated time with Will and me, providing them with experiences that they would have never had without the painful separation from all they knew and understood. The steps of trust Laney and Hank walked gave them more than they could have imagined. God is like that; He wants to give us, HIS children, good and perfect gifts above and beyond anything we can imagine. Even in times of painful adjustment and loss, we can trust Him; we can know that He is mindful of us and that He sees the big picture and knows that a time will come that we will be able to look back and see the gifts in the journey!

As we approached our departure date, I felt compelled to write regularly about our experiences, thoughts and feelings. I didn't want to forget what I learned, and I wanted to share my journey with others so they would be able to better understand the people of Afghanistan and pray for them. The pages that follow are the actual letters written to family and friends during our time in Afghanistan, a "real time" account of our experiences, hopes, fears, joys, and lessons learned. After each letter are reflections, thoughts and information that I wrote after returning home. I am honored to share my journey and new perspectives in the hope that you will see the "Roses in the Dust," not only in Afghanistan but in the garden in which the Lord has planted you.

Afghanistan 101

Afghanistan is a place that has had a history of conflict and war for centuries. Its geographical location—between the Middle East and Asia—as well as the tremendous richness of the land and the diversity of culture and ethnicity have contributed to this history. A brief summation of key historical events as well as a short explanation of some of the cultural and religious aspects of this intriguing country will lay a framework to help understand my experiences and perspectives as we lived in this beautiful and harsh land.

Afghanistan was not always broken and backwards; there was a time when Kabul was a modern, thriving city, rich in culture and education. During the 60's and 70's, Afghanistan was visited by thousands of young foreign men and women wanting to explore this rich cultural environment. Many would backpack over the mountains from one side to the other. At that time, the president of Afghanistan was enamored with John F. Kennedy and desired to model his country after what he saw in America. During this time, it was not unusual to see Afghan families looking more Western than Afghan. It was common and expected that most young people would attend one of several prestigious universities and would be expected to work in professional jobs. The chadar (head covering) was not required, and it was not unusual to see young women on the college campuses wearing short skirts, knee high boots, and having their hair uncovered. Not until the Russian armies invaded and destroyed their beautiful city did things begin to regress. Below is a simplified account of Afghan history. It is a dark and bloody history that has helped to shape the backward society of modern Afghanistan.

Afghanistan Timeline

300's BC	*Alexander the Great used Afghanistan as the Gateway to India.*
700's:	*Islamic conquerors*
1200-1400's:	*Genghis Khan and Tamerlane conquered the country.*
1839–1842:	*Anglo-Afghan War 1*
1878–1880:	*Anglo-Afghan War 2*
1893:	*UK established an unofficial border separating Afghanistan from British India.*
1919:	*Afghanistan became independent.*
1926:	*Emir Amanullah founded an Afghan monarchy.*
1950's:	*Afghanistan developed close ties with the Soviet Union during the cold war.*
1978:	*Military coup, Afghanistan became a Marxist regime.*
1979:	*Soviets launched an invasion of Afghanistan.*
1989:	*Soviet withdrawal*
1992:	*Islamic rebellion - fighting between rebel groups*

1996:   *A group of Islamic students calling itself the Taliban seized control of Kabul.*

1996:   *The Taliban took over the government of Afghanistan, but the government was only recognized by Pakistan, Saudi Arabia, and the United Arab Emirates.*

August 20, 1998:   *U.S. cruise missiles struck a terrorist training complex in Afghanistan believed to have been financed by Osama bin Laden.*

September 2001:   *Anti-Taliban guerrilla leader Ahmed Shah Massoud, of the group referred to as the Northern Alliance, was killed by suicide bombers.*

September 11, 2001:   *Taliban terrorist—al-Qaeda members— attacked New York's World Trade Center Towers and the Pentagon.*

October 7, 2001:   *The Taliban refused to turn over bin Laden, and the U.S. and its allies began daily air strikes against Afghan military installations.*

December 7, 2001:   *The Taliban regime collapsed.*

December 2001:   *Afghanistan interim government was formed.*

June 2002:   *Hamid Karzai became President.*

2002 – 2003:   *Peacekeeping forces entered the country.*

March 2003:   *International offensive against Kandahar and al-Qaeda members was launched.*

August 2003:   *NATO assumed command of peacekeeping troops.*

January 4, 2004:   *A new constitution was introduced.*

April 2004:	*International offensive along the Pakistan border against al-Qaeda members.*
2005	*Taliban insurgency renewed.*
2006	*President Bush visited Afghanistan.*
2010	*President Obama sent in 33,000 additional troops.*
2011	*Osama bin Laden was killed in Pakistan.*

The history of Afghanistan is one riddled with war and conflict. Some of the conflict is over the geographical location of the country, making Afghanistan a potential military "prize" for the bordering countries. However, much of the conflict in this land has arisen within its own people groups, all striving for religious and political gain. The country of Afghanistan has been in some type of civil war for centuries.

People Groups of Afghanistan

The Pashtun are the largest people group of Afghanistan and, by some estimations, the largest Muslim tribal group in the entire world. In appearance, the Pashtun most resemble Arabs. Most have dark hair and dark eyes and typically wear the traditional turban headscarf. The majority of Pashtun believe they are the elite of the Muslim faith, also believing that Islam was birthed from the Pashtun tribe. Pashtun are primarily Sunni Muslims, who are part of the branch of Islam that adheres to the orthodox tradition and acknowledges the first four caliphs (political and spiritual leaders) as rightful successors of Mohammed.

The second largest people group is the Tajiks, though some speculate they have surpassed the Pashtun in numbers.

Most Tajiks are Sunni Muslims and speak Persian; they are considered the closest rivals to the Pashtuns.

The Hazara are the third largest group and are believed to be descendants of Genghis Khan. Most Hazara have an Asian or Mongolian appearance. Usually Hazara men cannot grow beards and have very little body hair, supporting the belief that the Pashtun are more religiously elite since they can grow long heavy beards, believed to be a sign of fundamental Islam in that part of the world. Hazara are usually Shia Muslims who belong to the branch of Islam comprising sects believing in Ali and the Imams as the only rightful successors of Mohammed and in the concealment and messianic return of the last recognized Imam (spiritual leader). Because the Hazara are mostly Shia in a Sunni world and their physical features are so Asian, the Hazara are considered the lowest on the cultural hierarchy. The Hazara have been fighting for cultural equality and against prejudice for centuries.

There are more people groups living in Afghanistan, but these three comprise the highest percentage of the population. Each of these three people groups is located in specific geographical areas of Afghanistan, usually separated by distinct borders. However, living in Kabul, we had the opportunity to live and work with all three groups on a daily basis. In fact, within the organization in which we worked, all three people groups were represented. This is uncommon, and it is even more unusual that the individuals from these groups worked well with one another. The six men and one woman on our staff worked together every day and considered themselves to be like a family. Any one of them would willingly put their lives at risk for the sake of any of their coworkers, including William and me.

I believe the reason that the people working with us, from a variety of ethnic groups and tribal areas, displayed a level of commitment to one another and degree of mutual respect was in a direct correlation to the love of God permeating our organization. Though our entire staff was Muslim, most of the people coming and going through the house were Christians. God's love and peace blanketed our home and lives, and I believe directly affected the employees.

Paradise...Maybe

Islam is all about "works." If individuals follow certain guidelines and do everything the Koran teaches, then maybe Allah will allow them into Paradise. Notice, I said "maybe." There are no guarantees. If Afghans are asked if they will go to Paradise when they die, they will respond with, "I hope so, if Allah wills." I once asked an Afghan friend whether a person who does everything the Koran teaches and abides by all the rules of Islam was assured of Paradise. My friend answered "No, only if Allah wills. We hope the good deeds of our lives will balance the scales, and Allah will have mercy on us." So really, Islam is a big gamble. No wonder people are afraid. It's hard to imagine, but even in acts of charity and kindness, Afghans are motivated only in the hopes that they will be noticed by Allah. There is often very little respect for human life and the suffering of others; but if Allah sees that his followers have not given to the poor or shared their lives with those less fortunate, they will be punished for it.

One Afghan told my husband that Muslims even believe that if a Muslim builds a bridge during his life, every good deed of those who pass over that bridge will be accredited to the builder, even after his death. So there is not even an assurance that good deeds will be credited to the one performing them and not to others. Because of this fatalistic view, there is a strange mix of fear, selfishness, dishonesty, and corruption in this culture. One prevailing attitude is that if Muslims do enough good deeds in life, they can do anything else they want. However, because of the inability to "do" enough on their own to guarantee the favor of Allah, they often feel hopeless to live a "good enough" life.

PART TWO

The Journey in Real Time – Letters to Home

CHAPTER 3 - Laying the Foundation

Psalm 62:8

Trust in Him at all times; pour out your heart before Him; God is a refuge for us.

Letter 1 - Six Weeks and Counting

Six weeks and counting! It is hard to believe we are here. It seems like it was just yesterday when we could barely let ourselves wonder about the possibility of this adventure, and now we are a few weeks away from putting our suitcases on a plane and heading to a foreign land we'll call home. I remember our first encounter with this forgotten country almost five years ago; I came home from that very difficult trip exhausted, and as I sat in my big green devotional chair, I asked God what in the world He wanted me to do with all the things I had just seen and experienced. I remember saying, "Lord, what do you want me to do? I can't go back and live there. I can't do anything to help these forgotten people. Where do I put the horrific tales of destruction I have heard? Where do I put the devastation I have seen? I can't just stand in the line at the grocery store buying my four different kinds of coffee and act as if I deserve the life I live. It's only by Your grace that I am here and not there." As I sat, a thought swelled inside of me until I finally recognized it was the voice of the Lord saying, "Don't do anything with it. Just remember, and be a voice for those who have none." I tucked that command away in my heart, never thinking that the Lord would allow me to someday return to that broken country.

From that time on, I have had many opportunities to share the stories of Afghanistan, to tell others that there are precious people on the other side of the world that need our help. I, however, never dreamed that I would be able to be a part of that help. I feel incredibly honored to be asked to participate in this journey, humbled but honored; and I look forward to the things I will learn, receive and experience there and hope that I can take something of value to share with them as well.

So as the countdown has begun, our days are filling up with details that need our attention…housing, visas, school, travel, etc.; items that need to be bought, and people that we need to see. Laney and I have been practicing our hijab tying and picking out all the wonderful scarves we get to wear daily as we walk to and from school and the markets. Laney and I have also had to adapt our wardrobes as we prepare to pack our suitcases. We have replaced our capris and shorts and sleeveless shirts with floor-length skirts and long-sleeved blouses. Our outside wear also will consist of an abaya (overcoat) that we will wear with our hijabs anytime we are outside of our home or the school. I have also traded in my blond, highlighted, short haircut for a solid auburn color that William will help touch up each month as I grow my hair out.

As I write these words, I am filled with excitement and nervousness — excited to be going, excited to experience a new culture and learn about such beautiful people, excited to see how my days will fill themselves, and excited to see the amazing plans of our Father come to fruition. At the same time, I am quite nervous about all the unknowns, meeting new people, fitting into a new culture made up of both nationals and foreigners — nervous that the kids might not fit in or like their new school, nervous that I might not always be motivated by love and compassion but rather walk in my flesh and its desires, and nervous that I might not know how to support and help my amazing husband as he takes on such a big and important job. I'm also filled with mixed emotions about leaving my big kids behind. We have never been separated so far for so long before. All the kids are at very different seasons of their lives: Mitchell just starting college, Joy just getting the hang of it, Alex just finishing, and Emma working and caring for all our responsibilities here. So many things and so many details to consider. What amazing young women and men they have become. I am so honored to be their mother and so excited to see what great and mighty things lie ahead for them.

"God is my portion and my strength," all I need for today and tomorrow!

Personal Reflection

As I prepared to embark on this most unusual journey, I had to learn to balance two worlds: the world of the West, where more than half of our children and extended family would live; and a world unlike any I had ever experienced before, backward and unfamiliar, rough and unforgiving, beautiful and mysterious.

I spent hours researching, learning the culture and religion of my new home. I wrote foreigners living there trying to learn what to take and what I could buy there, asking questions about cooking, shopping and navigating a culture that is unsupportive of women outside of the home.

I also spent hours purging and organizing my American home, getting it ready to be left for a year. I tried to plan ahead for birthdays and special events. I made lists of things for our kids to know: numbers, names and places that would be important in the months to come. It was both exhausting and invigorating at the same time. I felt alive with purpose and clarity. I had so much to learn!

In America, the availability of "things" and the conveniences we have grown accustomed to really do breed attitudes of entitlement instead of gratitude. During our time in Afghanistan, I became so grateful for the "little things"—an occasional Diet Coke, good-smelling soap, a hamburger—things in my home country that seem like a right, not a privilege.

I remember going to market one day and finding a familiar cleaning product from America. There were only a few bottles, so I bought them up and probably paid way too much for them. That simple bottle of good smelling cleaner became the bright side of many a day. Because of the dust and dirt in Kabul, it was necessary to clean every day, wiping down everything. Kabul has the highest level of feces content in the air of any other country in the world and all of that feces-filled dust lands on the furniture and bedding every day, even with the windows shut. I would often feel a bit discouraged about this aggravating inconvenience until I brought out the lavender all-purpose cleaner; it reminded me of home and made my house smell amazing. Because I never knew if I would ever find the same thing more than once at market, I would dilute the solution. Even so, I felt like I was on top of the world every time I sprayed that bottle of cleaner.

In America, there are so many cleaning products that shopping can seem like a nightmare. Why do we really need twelve different types of all-purpose cleaners? The word "need" is the key, isn't it? We really don't "need" so many choices; yet it is those very choices that make us feel free, while at the same time, they make life more complicated. In a country where there are few choices, I became so grateful for the little things life offered—the Diet Coke I enjoyed once a day, occasional ice cubes, a warm shower, electricity, and running water. I woke every day thanking the Lord for basic things, shelter and food.

Thinking back, I remember vividly when we headed to the airport to say our goodbyes and start the adventure of a lifetime. As I watched my husband put suitcases on the scales, I couldn't help but reflect on what a crazy, decadent life we Americans live. Here I was moving to the other side of the universe with nine suitcases for four people. I left behind a three-story house filled with "things" I would rarely think of during our time away. How can we be so content to live with so little in one culture and constantly be striving for more in another? There would be so many times in the months to come that I would reflect on this question. Our lives in Afghanistan would prove to be so simple and sweet, so uncomplicated, so basic.

As I boarded the plane to leave, I had no idea how life would change for me. I had little perspective of what it would be like to live in a Muslim country as a Christian woman, to have no freedoms and opportunities of my own apart from my husband. I had no concept of what it would be like to be a prisoner in my own home, to be looked at like a piece of property instead of a human being. I had no grasp of how Islam had played such a huge role in oppressing the development of Afghanistan for centuries. I had no real clarity of the driving forces behind the tribal civil war that bubbled and flowed like hot lava ready to spew on unexpecting men, women and children. There was no way for me to sympathize with the broken hearts of mothers as they watched child after child die of simple correctable illnesses and malnutrition, or sisters and mothers, even husbands, as they watched mother after mother die in childbirth. I could not feel the hopelessness of young girls sold into marriage before puberty to pay for their brothers' schooling. How could I comprehend the fear and oppression that each Afghan goes through each day knowing that at any moment their homes and livelihoods could be blown to shreds? How could I grasp the hunger that gnaws in stomachs of children as they go to bed each night? I couldn't understand what it was like to shiver all night from the cold. How could I imagine the conversations I would have with the young women doctors about what it's like to marry for love and live not fearing that their husband would beat them every night? How could I know that I would love these people so much that my heart would break for them daily? How could I know that through this wonderfully raw and unexpected journey, I would glimpse the heart of God, see His love and desperation not only for the people of Afghanistan, but for me as well.

As I flew over the United States, then Europe and landed in the world's most decadent city, Dubai, I had no understanding that one more plane ride would plant me in the middle of the moon (or what would seem like the moon as it was so far from my perspective of life that I felt as if I had left our planet altogether).

In the weeks and months that followed my arrival on the moon, God went to work changing my perspective on almost every aspect of life. He changed the way I saw the world, my family and my life. The process would prove to be exciting, wonderful, painful, and sometimes nearly unbearable; but through it all, God did a creative miracle in me that I would experience a hundred times over.

James 4:6
But He gives more grace. Therefore He says: "God resists the proud, but gives grace to the humble."

Letter 2 - Time Ticking On

As the time ticks on, life here at the Brynn home is getting pretty crazy. We said goodbye to Mitchell this weekend as he headed off to college. Though it's the fourth time we have done this, it never gets easier and with us leaving the country in a few short weeks, the goodbyes were extra hard. So as I begin this week, I have a graduated daughter adjusting to being the main caretaker of all of our belongings as well as taking care of her siblings, a son leaving for college to finish his senior year and embark on grown-up life, a daughter adjusting to her second year of college and finding her way in her newly declared major, and a son leaving home for the first time and adjusting to life on the other side of the U.S. I also have a son and daughter preparing to leave for life in another country. Along with all the details of relocating, I am sorting through things to pack, saying goodbyes and walking through the details of school abroad, visas, travel details, security details and life away from more than half of my family. I have to admit that I have a lot feelings swirling around inside of me right now!

Personal Reflection

As I think back on this time, it's hard for me to believe that I was able to just pack up and leave four of our children behind. God's grace was so abundant in my life, not just for me but for my kids as well. We dialogued about the transition often, but all of my children are pretty quiet about their feelings. As I think back, I can't imagine what was going on inside their heads. Their parents were heading off to a war zone leaving them behind to take care of themselves. I know they all had doubts about the whole thing, but they never let it show. They all were in agreement that what we were doing was God's will for our family, and they were willing to make the sacrifices needed.

While we were gone, our oldest daughter Emma was in charge of all our bills and upkeep in the house as well as taking care of our two Great Danes. Emma was thrown into a world far beyond her years and was forced to live and take care of responsibilities foreign to her. Through all the months we were gone, Emma never complained, though I know she felt overwhelmed. While taking care of our life, Emma was also learning to navigate through a new job, Bible school, and being available to her siblings.

This journey stretched all of us and taught us that with the Lord, we can do all things. The moment we told them we were leaving them behind, the four older children had to grow up a few years really fast. As the days turned into weeks and months, I watched my children grow and mature. I continually gave them over to the Lord and asked Him to protect and teach them. The Lord is faithful; His mercy and grace are new each and every day.

When the Lord calls, He also equips. He gives grace and provides. Each of our children had to learn to hear His voice and rely on Him in new ways. Their faith and commitments were stretched and their abilities challenged. The Lord used this time and these situations to refine and adjust us all, using each of our individual journeys as the backdrop for each of our own stories.

Lamentations 3:22-23
Through the Lord's mercies we are not consumed,
because His compassions fail not. They are new
every morning; great is Your faithfulness.

Letter 3 - A Dose of Reality

If you were to walk into my bedroom today, you would be met with piles of clothes, books, winter coats, boots, suitcases, and bags of life's most important things. As I begin the sorting process and packing of these items, I am reminded of how excessively we Americans live. The thought of us living for the next year with only what we can take in our suitcases is a bit overwhelming until I stop and think, "What is 'need,' really?" Need is so relative, isn't it? How can I justify "needing" special coffee creamer or chocolate chips or my favorite lavender scented soap when most of the people living in my new country have never seen or experienced any of those things? How can I give so much attention and thought to what we will wear when there are children there who walk through the snow without shoes?

Need is relative for sure, and God is helping me to put life into perspective as I walk through this journey. There is a "need" for me to simplify and really consider what is most important. This journey will be an exercise in keeping life in perspective. I don't believe that God wants us to all live a life of poverty, but I do believe that we should strive to keep His perspective continually before us. The pressure of American culture is overwhelming, the bombardment of advertising and affluence and the "need" to satisfy our every whim just because we can. As an exercise, just stand in your local grocery store sometime and take a look around. The amount of "stuff" is completely overwhelming. Do we really "need" 25 different varieties of everything from coffee to bread? We are all so spoiled and so caught up in the excess that we can't focus on what is most important. As my time gets closer to leaving, I am trying to spend more time reflecting on these things, determining to be so very grateful for what we have and to recognize that maybe one of the reasons we are blessed with so much is to have the ability to give it away and not just hoard it for ourselves.

As I am preparing, I am sorting my piles over and over, each time asking the question, "Do I really "need" this, or do I just want it because I am fearful of doing life without it?" As my piles get smaller, there is a load that gets lighter on my shoulders. There is liberty in freeing oneself from the stuff of life. With a family of eight, there is just a lot of "stuff" that has to swirl in our lives, stuff that I can't always control. I can, however, be conscious of the "stuff" and purpose to evaluate its meaning in our lives.

Personal Reflection

The lesson of simplification is one that the Lord worked to teach me for the entire time we lived in Afghanistan and still continues today. I have to admit that I loved my little house and simple life in Kabul and feel that it was a gift the Lord gave me to help me redefine life. I was astonished how many times I would go about my day in my tiny apartment and never think of my house and "stuff" in America. I had all I needed to live a full and happy life within the three little rooms of our apartment. What in the world did I need with all that "stuff" back in my house in the West? During this process, I learned to hold on to things lightly and reevaluate everything that came into my life. It was an ongoing challenge even while I was living in Afghanistan. You may think, "How can stuff 'own you' in Afghanistan? There is nothing there." Well, human nature is human nature, and we all have a desire to surround ourselves with "things" that make us feel good. Even in Kabul there is a risk of letting "stuff" own you. Because of the constant transition of foreigners in Afghanistan, almost every weekend there is a garage sale where people on their way out are trying to get rid of stuff.

One of my favorite things to do with our housemates was to go to these garage sales and see what "American" treasure we could find. At times I would laugh looking through and wanting to buy the very things I had weeded out in America before leaving. I always felt a bit of a panic thinking, "Oh my, what if I need this sometime and can't find it again?" If a person is not careful, one can become a hoarder of stuff even in Kabul.

Understand my heart: there is a balance that has to be found. When living on the foreign field, it's very difficult emotionally if you do not surround yourself with familiar things. In my case, I am not Afghan and probably couldn't thrive if I lived like an Afghan. I am American, and the Lord understands that. Having things in my home that reminded me of America and my family was a healthy thing. What is not healthy is when that stuff begins to "own" me, and I have more attachment to the things than I should.

No matter where we live or what conditions we live in, there is always a risk of "stuff" becoming too important to us. One of my favorite things is having wonderfully scented candles around my house. I love the way they look, and the smell is comforting and uplifting to me. In Kabul, there are no nice smelling candles; there are plain wax ones that are used when the lights go out, but none used as decoration. I took several with me when we went, but candles are heavy and my weight allowance and space was limited. As I started going to the garage sales, I began a process of "hoarding" scented candles. It got to be a bit crazy actually; if I found one, even if it was half burned, I would have to buy it. I ended up with several plastic containers full after a few months. One day I remember cleaning and looking at my candle stash thinking, "Really? Does anyone really need this many candles?" It was a small thing, but it represented a larger one—a process of justification in my life where I could rationalize my way into whatever I wanted. The Lord used the exercise to help make me sensitive to things around me that were taking my attention and focus. This process of evaluation is something that continues in my life on a daily basis. When I returned home to America and my house of "stuff," I was again faced with the same questions. It is a process that I think will be ongoing in my life. I hope that as I continue to grow and mature, "stuff" will have less and less of a hold on me.

Mark 10:29-30

So Jesus answered and said, "Assuredly, I say to you, there is no one who has left house or brothers or sisters or father or mother or wife or children or lands, for My sake and the gospel's, who shall not receive a hundredfold now in this time--houses and brothers and sisters and mothers and children and lands, with persecutions--and in the age to come, eternal life.

Letter 4 - To Veil or Not to Veil?

These past few weeks have been filled with reading and studying about our new home: the people, the language, the culture, the history, etc. As I am learning about these amazing people and their lives, I am taken aback at how much I am learning about myself. Misconceptions and prejudices I didn't know I had, not only about our new country but my country of origin as well; misconceptions about humanity in general. Some of the things I am seeing I am ashamed to have found. God is keeping before me the foundational truth that we are all made in His image, and we are all loved the same. It's only by grace that we have the life that we do. It really has nothing to do with our intellect or gifts or abilities or worth; it only has to do with God's goodness. How blessed we are to have been given the opportunity to know and see the truth! How rich we all would be to keep that truth before us!

As I have been sorting the things to pack and reading the information about our new country, I am also having an opportunity to see things a bit differently in regard to how I, as a woman, am expected to dress and act in my country of origin and in Afghanistan. On first impression, it would be very easy to see the customs and practices of my new country as oppressive and cruel; and, yes, the extremes of the fundamental beliefs are most certainly that. I am, however, also inclined to say that the extremes of our own country are oppressive and cruel as well. The expectations of the U.S. as to how a woman

36

should act and dress is, to me, quite overwhelming, unrealistic and oppressive in regard to how I feel I was created to live. The expectation of proving how independent and capable we are by showing as much skin as we can, becoming pushy and loud and determined to compete with men in every arena of life has, I think, made us less feminine, has hardened our hearts, made us insecure, and caused us to strive to prove ourselves. It is no wonder that my new country sees those views and expectations as part of the thinking of a godless society. Maybe we are becoming that. In Afghanistan, the veiling of women, in most cases, is not seen as oppressive, but for the security and safety of the women. Even just adhering to the "modest" code of dress of Islam takes a huge pressure off of the female population. By modestly adorning themselves, women are free to go about their duties without the men staring and gawking at them. Think about the contrast of how a young woman here in the U.S. would dress to go to the mall and how a young woman in Afghanistan would dress to go to her market. Honestly, it's embarrassing to consider. I am not opposed at all to going and living in a country where my young teenage daughter is expected to keep her skin and curves covered. Again, let me point out that there are extremes of both thoughts, and I am not in agreement with either. I do see them as oppressive and cruel; but at the same time, I am willing to consider that there is some truth and wisdom in the fundamental belief in modesty and am looking forward to living in a culture where my young daughter and I do not have to live under the pressure of looking "perfect" and constantly having to fight the lines between appropriate and inappropriate.

Personal Reflection

I loved wearing the Muslim hijab (the traditional overcoat and head covering worn by Muslim women) while living in Afghanistan. That may seem weird, especially when it has such a negative connotation here in America. I wore it out of choice, not because a father or husband or religion commanded me to, so that makes a difference. In Afghanistan, foreign women are a novelty and stand out wherever they are. Wearing the hijab caused me to blend in a bit more and made me feel more a part of the culture. The hijab gave me a "sisterhood" of sorts with the local women that transcended language, education, nationality and religion. Coming from a culture that celebrates and emphasizes the shape of a woman's body, I found great relief and peace that I was now expected to keep my curves hidden. I truly wish there was more of a modest element in the West; things are way out of control here.

My favorite part of the hijab is the headscarf, or chadar. I have quite a collection of beautiful scarves and often had to reevaluate my collection (like my candles), so it didn't get out of hand. The headscarf is the one thing women can use to express their personalities and style. The colors are vibrant and the patterns beautiful. Unlike other Muslim countries where women are expected to wear black all of the time, in Afghanistan it is completely acceptable to wear a wide variety of colors and textures.

The last thing I would put on before leaving my apartment would be my chadar; and though all women wear them, it was something that made me unique and special as an individual. Many foreigners hate the chadar; it's hot and bothersome and to some felt like a cruel rule. For me though, it gave me a connection to the culture and women that I embraced and enjoyed.

I remember when we were heading home to America for good, and we landed in Dubai; I felt the pain of grief and sadness that it was time to pack my chadar away for good. It was a personal link I had to the culture and people of Afghanistan, and I wasn't ready to give it up yet. It was a weird feeling to know that a simple piece of cloth was so vitally important and necessary in one place in the world and yet had no significance or meaning in another. What had come to be my safety and comfort in a strange and harsh place was now just a piece of cloth, an accessory, in a drawer. Packing my hijab away began a hard time of grieving for me as I left behind the things that over the past year had been tattooed on my heart.

Many people have asked me what would have happened if I had chosen not to wear the hijab while living in Afghanistan. Is it a law to wear the hijab? Would I go to jail if I didn't wear it? No, it's not a law—not for foreigners anyway; and no, I would not have been sent to jail. However, as a woman, it would have been very difficult to live in this Muslim culture and have any kind of effective or authentic relationships without the head covering and abaya (a loose-fitting full-length robe worn by some Muslim women). Islam is an extremely conservative religion which teaches that a woman should cover herself modestly so as not to cause men to stumble. In Afghanistan, this is taken to an even greater extreme because the people have a great fear of the Taliban and of violating the rules they imposed on women when they were in control. Before the Taliban came into power, the oldest male in each household determined how much a woman was to veil. There is still great debate among Muslims about the extent to which a woman should veil or cover and who should make the decision. In Afghanistan, it is usually decided by the oldest male in the family before a woman is married and by the mother-in-law or husband after she marries.

As a foreign woman living in Afghanistan, I believe it was very important to respect and uphold the cultural and religious practice of veiling. To show honor and respect in this manner goes a long way in creating relationships. During our time in Afghanistan, there were only a few foreign women I saw without at least a head covering and those not wearing them were most certainly looked down upon by the Afghans. It is difficult for many foreign women to understand how important this is because we come from cultures where free will and choice are rights, not privileges, granted. It is tempting to rebel against the strong oppression of women. Most women raised in a free society might be inclined to feel entitled to live and act the way they want with no consideration for the nationals and their traditions and beliefs. It doesn't take long in Afghanistan to know that this prideful attitude usually just leads to trouble.

There is a mystery surrounding women in the Afghan culture. Islam teaches that all women should cover themselves, deemphasizing the shape and curve of the female body and not revealing any skin that could be considered erotic or enticing to men. If there is ever a situation where a man is caught in adultery or fornication with a woman, it will always be the woman who is blamed and never the man. In such cases, it is always understood that the woman has done something to entice or seduce the man, including instances of rape. The man is never at fault because it is believed the woman forced him to do what he did. Sound familiar? That rationale goes all the way back to the garden where Satan presented that argument as a counterfeit to God's truth. Men have been using it ever since.

In most Islamic cultures, until a man marries, he has never even seen a woman's bare arm with the exception of perhaps a sister or mother. Men spend most of their time trying to imagine what women look like under their flowing abayas and hijabs. Most men and women are kept separated even within their own household. Men and women don't eat together or sleep in the same room. They are segregated socially and, unless permitted, men are never allowed to have a conversation with any woman other than a family member. Even weddings are completely segregated affairs. Weddings are celebrated in large wedding halls where men celebrate on one side of a wall and women on another. Eating, dancing, and socializing happen only with those of the same gender; it is never appropriate for men and women to celebrate together.

Most Muslims, including Afghan Muslims, consider Christians to be infidels (ones without faith). From a Muslim's perspective, American Christians are godless and immoral. After living in Afghanistan for a while, I quickly began to understand why they have this view of us. Muslims live by a strict rule of modesty both for men and women. Women and men alike wear long sleeves and long pants or skirts. Even if a woman is wearing a skirt, she will also wear a pair of pants or leggings underneath just in case the skirt is ever lifted or shifts, revealing any part of her leg. Sometimes for men but always for women, it is inappropriate to wear a shirt that does not cover her backside or her chest past the collarbone. Showing a woman's curves is considered inappropriate and a woman doing so is asking for trouble. In some places, Afghanistan included, a woman will wear a long overcoat called an abaya over her regular clothes just to ensure her silhouette is shapeless and does not attract attention.

Since the invasion by the Russians in December of 1979, followed by Taliban rule, Afghanistan was virtually cut off from the rest of the world. There was very little media or news allowed in. During the Taliban's reign, all forms of media were considered illegal. All televisions, radios, and tapes were destroyed along with all books and any other form of information transfer. The already information-starved country regressed even farther into the darkness of ignorance. For almost thirty years now, the Afghans have known very little of the world outside its borders. When the Taliban was run out of the country and the U.S. military took over the security, a huge influx of modern technology made its way into the hands of the common family. Televisions came first and then computers and cell phones. Along with this technology came the revelation of how most of the rest of the world lives, or at least what the Afghans perceive to be how we live. With television came MTV and the Hollywood perspective of love and romance. With computers came pornography. It is no wonder Afghans think foreigners are infidels. If I saw nothing but MTV and Hollywood on television, and the men in my household now had free access to pornography, I would think we were a country without faith, too. Maybe we are.

1 Peter 3:3-4

Do not let your adornment be merely outward—arranging the hair, wearing gold, or putting on fine apparel—rather let it be the hidden person of the heart, with the incorruptible beauty of a gentle and quiet spirit, which is very precious in the sight of God.

Letter 5 - I Now Have Two Houses

Well it's official; I have a house on the other side of the world. Not at all what a person would envision for a second home and certainly not the location most would pick, but prime real estate nonetheless. Housing in K-Town is very hard to come by, at least if you want a house with running water, electricity, and all its windows intact. Finding a house is one thing, but finding a fair landlord is another. When you make a decision to move to Afghanistan, you can't just call and ask your trusty realtor to spend the day with you walking through your options. Options? Again, "relative." I think, "What do I really need?" A kitchen would be good, a bathroom even better, certainly one that we can shower in; okay, maybe the shower thing is pushing it. I'll take a bathtub! A separate room to sleep in would be nice and another for the kids is even better! I'm all for closeness, but the American custom of your kids sleeping in a separate room would be hard to compromise on. So, kitchen, bedroom, and bathroom - that certainly feels like need; but again, it's relative when your neighbors are living 12 in a one-room house all sleeping on the floor and cooking on a stove in the middle of the room that also doubles as their heat. Bathroom? Oh yeah; walk through the snow several hundred yards behind the house. Okay, so we have established need. What about location, location, location? The two most important places to be close to are school and work. Well, not easy when school is a fifteen minute drive from the hospital. Since we won't have a car and riding in public transportation is not an option because of security issues, our feet will be the best form of getting from one place to another. This could also be an issue because women can't walk down the street without an escort. Walking for long periods of time and over great distances is not recommended because of security and/or underground mines.

After lots of emails and sorting through details, our housing situation is a miracle. We will be living on the second story of a two-story house sharing the space with another expatriate couple working there with a water purification project. The second story has been converted into a small apartment, complete with a kitchen, a living room, two bedrooms, and a bathroom. There is a small fenced yard where the kids can be outside and a basement with a Wii. The best part of the situation is that it is only two hundred yards from the kids' school. We will all be able to walk to school together each morning and afternoon. Laney will only have to wear her hijab until she enters the school; then she will be free to act and dress as most Western children do...well, a modified modest version of most Western teenagers.

My husband will have a private driver pick him up each day along with a work colleague who lives several blocks away. The driver will drive my husband to work each day and drop him off at our front door when the day is done.

So we have a house, but what about things to put into it? Think about furnishing your new home here in the states—the time, the money, the attention—and then think about doing it all sight unseen via email. I'm not talking about internet ordering and shipping. I'm talking about buying from individuals, piece by piece, or waiting until you get there and trying to find it on the streets. That is what most people have to do when they relocate to Afghanistan. We, on the other hand, were contacted by a family who just left Kabul this spring and had a whole apartment of supplies they needed to sell. What a blessing! So, we purchased the package deal of kitchen supplies, furniture, linens, and appliances, all sight unseen. Some dear friends had it all transported to our new home where it sits waiting for us. I have to say, it's been a bit challenging to my Western mindset *thinking about setting up our new home with articles I have never seen before, wanting to make a house a home with things around me that match and have personal meaning; but God is teaching me to enjoy the hassle-free form of shopping, and I'm learning to trust that He knows what I like and would want and, yes, even need, more than I do! I am so excited to get there and see what God has done for us. My second home is not at the lake or on the beach, but it is in an exciting location; and it will be filled with love and warmth and gratitude for the "simple" things of life!*

Our children will be attending an English speaking, English curriculum international school. The school's population is made up of 85 percent Afghan students and 15 percent foreign children (American, European, Australian and Asian). The school is taught completely in English but does offer Dari as a language option. The kids will be able to participate in music, sports, drama, and dance while they are there, as well as having the amazing opportunity to interact with and learn about another culture. We are so excited about this opportunity for Laney and Hank and feel it will be one of the highlights of their lives. I will be volunteering as a substitute teacher, so I will have the opportunity to be involved in the kids' school life on a personal level. I am looking forward to getting back into the classroom after so many years and see this as the "icing on the cake" of a wonderful new adventure.

Personal Reflection

When we decided to move to Kabul, we worried about how Hank and Laney would adjust. They really had no choice but to go with us, and yet both were leaving behind meaningful relationships, activities and experiences that they would miss. Neither wanted to go, but both were willing and obedient and chose to trust us. It was our prayer that they would flourish and grow during our time away and not become resentful or bitter from the experience.

During our time in Kabul, we never heard either of them complain or whine and ask to go back home or be angry at us for making them move to Afghanistan. Though both had several experiences that could have given them much to complain about, they didn't; and when our time came to an end, both cried and asked if we could stay for another year. God's faithfulness is astounding. Not only did He protect, provide for and grace our children for the journey, but He gave both of them deep meaningful friendships and experiences that left their lives changed and their hearts linked forever to this most unlikely place and its people.

Laney and Hank's experiences at the international school proved to be another of God's rich and amazing gifts. The children's year experiencing a different culture, making friends from all over the world, and being challenged and pushed academically will be one that will shape and mold the thinking and choices of my children forever. The rich relationships made with people from a different religion and background were some of the sweetest to date. This experience opened my children's eyes to the needs of the world and turned their egocentric perspectives towards others. There were times that were challenging and testing to us all, but God was faithful to help us see His plans and purposes.

The first few months that the children were at school were a huge adjustment and learning curve for them. Both had to navigate through a security system with 12-foot walls and guards with machine guns. The children had to make new friends and learn a daily schedule foreign to them both. Being in junior high and making a transition like this is a tall order.

Early on it was especially difficult for our son. As it turned out, he was the only foreign boy in his class. All of the other boys were Afghan nationals. Now in the best of situations it can be difficult to navigate through a new school in the first year of junior high. But he had to do it alone with a group of boys with whom he didn't share a primary language and certainly didn't share the same life, culture or faith perspectives. During the first few weeks, the Afghan boys shoved, pushed, slapped and teased him regularly, unseen by the school authorities, of course.

When Hank came home one day with his jeans and gloves ripped from being tripped in PE class, I was ready to pack my bags and head back to America. I sat down with him and told him I was going to go to the school administration and maybe talk to a few of the boys as well. He begged me to stay out of it, saying that he wanted to handle it. Looking back, I can see how it was so important that we allowed him to work it out, as it would have likely made things worse if I had jumped in. In this culture, where respect for women is low, having a woman fight your battles is not a good idea. Hank said, "It's okay, Mom; I will just pray for them. I am sure it will get better." At that moment, it was like a slap in the face; praying for those boys was the last thing I wanted to do! But out of the mouth of my child had come words that spoke truth to me. Over the weeks to come we prayed for those boys. One day, after being hit in the back of the head again, Hank turned around and said, "If you want to be my friend, you will have to stop hitting me." The boy looked at him with a puzzled expression; but from that moment forward, the behavior stopped and a great friendship was forged with the boy and several other Afghan classmates. The boys were trying to build a relationship with Hank, but they didn't know how, having been raised in a harsh, violent society. Hank's God-given wisdom helped them to see the truth and led them all to a great relationship and friendship.

As I look back on the year though, I am astounded at the opportunities Laney and Hank ended up having. Both made wonderful friends and attended a youth group full of wonderful young men and women. Laney had the opportunity to take tap and ballet classes with some of the most qualified teachers I have ever met. She had the opportunity to help teach the younger girls, many of them Afghan. At the end of the year,

Laney danced in a recital at a level on par with anything I have seen. She would not have had this opportunity if we had not made this move.

Hank had the opportunity to play soccer with an Afghan team, playing teams with much older players. He was the only non-Afghan on the field! Not too many American boys can say that they had that opportunity.

The education that our kids received during this year was far better than we had ever expected. Both children were challenged and pushed harder academically than ever before. After returning home and entering back into their American school, both were above grade level in their academics. Who would ever imagine that moving to Afghanistan would advance my children culturally, athletically, academically and spiritually?

Romans 8:28

And we know that all things work together for good to those who love God, to those who are the called according to His purpose.

Letter 6 - The Last Push

Well, we are down to our last two weeks before leaving and in the middle of the last push to get everything done. At this point I have to ask myself, "Are we having fun yet?" Ummmm, the answer is, "NO!" Don't get me wrong; I'm still totally psyched about our adventure and can't wait to get the whole thing underway, but the preparation and details and "stuff" to do is just a downright drag! Just in case you are thinking that when a person makes a decision like this, and believes with her whole heart that it's the right decision, that everything will simply fall into place...WRONG! Often it can be quite the contrary. The work is huge, the distractions many, and the emotional toll draining! In the past two weeks, we have had three major appliances break, and the sump pump in our basement went out. The riding lawn mower broke, the transmission in one of our cars went out, and a set of dental retainers disappeared into thin air. On top of that, the house in Afghanistan we had secured and to which all of our newly purchased furniture has been moved has fallen through, and we are now homeless. Honestly, I know in my head that all these things are just distractions from the things we need to be concentrating on, and I know that God is bigger than anything that comes up. Even with the house situation, I know that if the situation we had secured is not right, there is simply something better—maybe better means a shower and heat. Knowing this in my head and walking it out are two different things though. I feel like I'm handling things fairly well and walking through all the motions of the day; but then out of the blue, I have a stomach ache and burst into tears during an episode of "Extreme Home Makeover" and can't stop the water works for an hour. I suppose if I would put our lives on a stress chart of change, it would be flashing red: two graduations, three kids leaving for college, one moving home, two kids in puberty, junior high craziness, some medical challenges, and a major move to a less than exotic location all in the last three months.

Okay; enough of the "Debbie Downer" stuff. I guess I just needed to vent a bit. Here are some bright spots in the situation. All the things that have broken in the last two weeks have happened now, and not while we were gone, and are fixed. We had a wonderful weekend visiting with family and friends who love and support and believe in us. More are coming this weekend. We are all healthy and strong and provided for. My kids are doing awesome. We have absolutely everything we need and almost everything we could want. Our visas were approved. Financial support is coming in; and though we are now off salary, God is still providing all we need. We have a place to stay for the first two weeks where we will be taken care of and trained to live in our new location. I receive cards and emails and calls from so many people every day giving me words of encouragement and support. I could go on and on, but I'm feeling so much better that I think I will just dwell on these things for awhile!

The last two weeks, along with lots of challenges, have also been filled with lots of learning about our new location. We have been in what our family is calling culture and religion school. We have been reading, dialoging, and watching teachings on the culture and beliefs of our new land; and we are learning so much. The similarities are many and the differences far less than I imagined for two countries so far apart in advances and beliefs and geography. I am gaining more love and respect daily for the people and customs of our new home. Ignorance does foster fear! Think about that for a moment — the more we don't really understand about certain things, the more room there is for our own prejudices and interpretations of truth. When we take the time to really learn and understand those around us, we are much more equipped to see the truth and remove our own opinions about things. There is room for relationship and growth, love and respect, and, hopefully, less room for fear, pride, and control. We should all strive to see people and situations without the filter of judgment propelled by pride and personal opinion. If we can see people for the "truth" of who they are — creations made by the Creator for good and perfect works, made in beauty and splendor, unique and wonderful, full of worth (worth like a precious gift) — then we can start at a place of hope and not fear. I am so grateful for this journey; hard and raw and painful at times, but so grateful nonetheless. I am moved to tears now, not from stress but from gratitude. What a wonderful gift we all have been given, being allowed to participate in the process of life full of relationships, growth, reconciliation, hope, love and, yes — heartache and pain.

I was reminded this weekend by a dear person in my life that we all have a purpose, a course, a destiny; and we need to be reminded to stay true to that purpose. We all have different things to do, but things nonetheless, and, in the big picture, all of great value. We need to stay focused on these purposes and committed to stay obedient to our course. People need us; we need each other. If we don't stay committed to do what we are designed to do, then people will suffer and things will be left undone. I want to commit to ask each day what my course is and what I am to be obedient in today and then have the grace to ask it again tomorrow! One of the biggest lessons right now is that I am learning to FIND ROSES IN MY OWN DUST!

Personal Reflection

God is so faithful; He did all this and more. This trip started a personal journey of opening my heart to the things of God, not just for the people of Afghanistan, but for me personally. It was a raw and sometimes difficult process filled with lonely days and feelings of inadequacy. Through the hard things, God showed Himself faithful and true and did it in a place I never expected. Because of the nature of the country and culture, I was forced to spend more time listening and learning than doing, something that is not easy for me. I learned to just be, instead of always trying to be more. I learned that God has a plan even in the silence, in what seems to be unproductive days. The Lord began teaching me about trust and peace on a whole new level. He taught me to have an awareness of Him in situations that seemed like, at first glance, He was not at work. He revealed to me a personal plan, not just a corporate one. He stripped back layers of distractions and crutches that I often gravitated to so that He could reveal Himself in a new way.

I am grateful for the hard things, the things that challenged and frustrated me, for in those things God became more. One scripture was very meaningful to me in the middle of all of this:

> *But He said to me, My grace, My favor and loving-kindness and mercy are enough for you, (that is, sufficient against any danger and enables you to bear the trouble manfully); for My strength and power are made perfect - fulfilled and completed and show themselves most effective - in (your) weakness. Therefore, I will all the more gladly glory in my weaknesses and*

infirmities, that the strength and power of Christ, the Messiah, may rest – yes, may pitch a tent (over) and dwell - upon me! 2 Corinthians 12:9 (Amplified)

God's strength is always there; but in my weakness, it is shown strong. In the difficult things, He is magnified and shows His glory.

Jeremiah 29:11
For I know the thoughts that I think toward you, says the Lord, thoughts of peace and not of evil, to give you a future and a hope.

CHAPTER 4 – Life on the Moon

Psalm 139:7–10

Where can I go from Your Spirit? Or where can I flee from Your presence? If I ascend into heaven, You are there; If I make my bed in hell, behold, You are there. If I take the wings of the morning, and dwell in the uttermost parts of the sea, even there Your hand shall lead me, And Your right hand shall hold me.

Letter 7 - Five Days

Wow! Five days until we leave. Hard to believe that after weeks of preparations and details we are finally at this point. We have nine suitcases packed, weighed, and re-weighed and still I lay in bed at night wondering what I have forgotten. I knew it was bad when, packing the last bag this week, I had to choose between hair color and chocolate because of weight and space. Well, let me tell you, that was no easy choice! In the end, the hair color won. I guess that means I am more vain than I thought. Now for those of you who know me and are worried for my family if I don't have chocolate, don't worry. I have divided it up into all our carry-ons! Come on, I know my limits! And for those of you wondering if I got the peanut butter in; well, you don't have to worry about that either; I found out I can buy it there! God is good, is He not?

As I'm writing this, the kids are sitting at the table doing school work, William is gone running errands, and the house is totally quiet; it's hard to hold back the tears as I reflect on so many things: saying goodbye to family and friends, thinking about leaving the comfort and peace of my home, wondering about all the unknowns. At the same time, I am moved to tears, not just about the hard things but about the good things that this journey brings, being grateful for this amazing journey, reflecting on the faithfulness of God, and being surrounded with the encouragement and support of so many people who love us; it's very humbling and wonderful.

I don't really know what the days and months will bring; but, really, do we ever? We think we do. We try to control and plan and schedule, but life still throws us curves. In some ways, being totally out of control has brought some rest and peace; no fretting over the calendar wondering how we can get everything in. Just an anticipation of what tomorrow holds. Maybe life would be richer and more wondrous if we could do that every day. The situation I find myself in takes away all sense of control. I don't have any idea what is around the corner or what the weeks will hold for us; but I do know that we will be together and that God is good and in control. That simple thought brings a lot of peace to my heart. I feel a lot more room being made in me to seek new and wonderful things each day, to see the big picture in life, and to learn to find roses in the midst of garbage and dirt. In a weird way, this adventure brings some of the things that our family finds on a vacation—three meals a day with Daddy, evenings filled with conversation and play instead of sports and school work, time to play games and enjoy each other, time to read and appreciate the quiet, and time for relationships. If I look at this adventure like that, I can't help but get excited and marvel at the goodness of God in all we have been given. Gratitude is the word for the week. I am focusing on gratitude for what I have, not sadness for what I am leaving behind.

I am looking forward to sharing with you the good, the bad, and the wonderful in the days and weeks ahead, and I look forward to seeing God's hand in every step of this journey. I hope to share with you the wonder of a culture and people not like ourselves, yet exactly like us. I look forward to giving all of you a glimpse into what lies outside of our borders and politics and, most of all, bridging the gulf between two worlds that are really not as different as we may think. So here is to adventure; here is to relationships, family, friends and life; and here is to the wonder of it all!

Personal Reflections

While we prepared to leave, I was catapulted in my mind back to an experience we shared five years earlier when I had visited Kabul for the first time. I will never forget leaving Afghanistan that day. The snow was falling, and temperatures were hovering around zero. My husband and I had gone through the two checkpoints to get to the main terminal. Our luggage had to be searched by hand, as there were no security x-ray machines. We pulled up to the terminal and the first thing I noticed was that the windows were either cracked or completely blown out and the snow was drifting inside. When we arrived just ten days earlier, I had not seen this part of the airport because we met our contacts right outside of the baggage area. Now, as we entered the terminal to await our departure, we were not even sure that our flight could depart because of the weather. Kabul sits in a bowl of beautiful snow-capped mountains and, though beautiful to look at and strategic to the security of the city, they do not make for good visibility for airplanes trying to fly in anything less than clear weather. We were scheduled to fly on an Afghan airline staffed with a Russian crew whose entire fleet had recently gone from three planes to one. The first plane had been grounded when the drunken pilot had tried to land the plane without lowering the landing gear. The second aircraft had flown into the side of the very mountains I had stood looking at through the windows just a week earlier, killing everyone, including several foreigners working in Kabul. The third was scheduled to arrive within the hour to take us to Dubai where we would catch our international flight.

For the next six hours we stood. We stood because there were no chairs in the terminal, only a set of stairs leading to an overlook on the second floor. For the majority of the time, it was just my husband and me in the terminal. At one point, I did catch a glimpse of a woman in a burka being escorted to a side room. My husband and I were standing on the stairway looking out the window at the snow. Actually, my husband was standing behind me a few steps, as culturally it was not acceptable for us to be standing side by side. Suddenly, a Humvee armored vehicle came screeching to a halt outside and four expat men in uniform jumped out with their machine guns pointed at the terminal. At the same exact time, six Afghan soldiers behind us on the landing of the second floor drew their guns. In that instant I heard my husband say, "If they start shooting, just hit the floor!" Of course, at that moment I lost all sensitivity to the cultural norms, turned to my husband and retorted, "Are you kidding me?! Did you just say that?!" It was like a scene in a movie all happening in slow motion. The very next moment, we intently watched as a plainclothes Afghan man approached the door where he was met by an Afghan soldier. They exchanged some words, and I saw the plainclothes man open his suit coat revealing three or four handguns strapped to his body. The soldier stepped aside and allowed the man through. The man calmly walked across the lobby and entered a room in the back of the terminal. The men outside and those above us relaxed and lowered their guns. At that moment, I just kept thinking, "I'm not in Kansas anymore, Toto!" immediately followed by the thought, "If we die, will anyone actually know?" It was a weird, surreal moment. It seemed like hours had passed, though I'm sure it was only a few minutes, as we stood there not knowing what to do and then watched as the plainclothes gentleman returned and left with his personal guards. We were told later that the group had arrived to escort a high profile Afghan general out of the airport.

Another hour or so passed before we were told we could enter the official waiting area to wait for our incoming flight, which we took to be a good sign that the aircraft would indeed arrive. (Of course, after living in Kabul for a year and flying in and out of the country several times, I now know that this could mean absolutely nothing.) When we walked through the door into the waiting area, I was astonished to find 150 or so Afghan and military men also waiting for this same flight. Where had these men been all this time? I looked around and saw only one other woman, an Afghan woman wearing a burka and sitting in the corner. The air was thick with cigarette smoke and not only smelled of cigarettes but also distinctly of livestock. Most of the Afghan men in the room were wearing the traditional turban and long robes of a shepherd. I'm sure they had left their sheep just hours earlier to board the plane that would be taking them on their first flight ever to Mecca, the land of "salvation" for most Muslims. I'm sure these men had been saving for this trip for years, and their families would go without many things so they could go and represent them to their "Holy Land." Most were carrying plastic bags instead of luggage and empty water bottles to be filled with "holy water" to carry back to their families and friends. The few foreigners in the room were most likely former military men working contractually for security companies guarding high profile people.

As we walked into the room, every eye turned and watched me walk across the waiting area to the window. As I passed, one Afghan man stood and blew his cigarette smoke in my face. I tried to ignore the heavy stares and uncomfortable feeling in the pit of my stomach. There were no seats available in the room and no man was going to give up his seat for a lowly foreign woman. We found a spot against the window in the corner directly under the "No Smoking" sign. Oh, the irony.

For the next two hours, we prayed and watched for the arriving plane. The snow was coming down like a heavy blanket, and we could hear the planes circling just above the clouds, only to fly off, unable to land. As we were praying, the clouds finally opened up like a window, and we saw the sun for the first time in days. Everyone in the room cheered and shouted as the airplane we had been waiting for dropped through the opening in the clouds and landed. The next thirty minutes were a blur as we were literally herded out the door into the blanket of snow to board the plane. The luggage was thrown into the bottom of the aircraft, and we finally started taxiing down the runway.

As the plane was moving toward the runway, I realized there were no trucks spraying de-icing liquid onto the wings of our aircraft. Then I realized for the millionth time, "Oh yeah, we are in Afghanistan." I began to pray more intensely. As the plane began to accelerate to navigate the steep climb over the mountain range, all the Afghan men jumped up out of their seats and rushed to the back of the aircraft. Because these men had never flown before and the instructions to "buckle your seatbelts" and "stay in your seat" were given in Russian (they all spoke Dari), they were panicked to realize the plane was leaving the ground.

It was complete mayhem as the stewardesses were yelling at the men to sit down, and the men were not listening; first, because foreign women were yelling at them, and second, because they had no idea what was happening. Fear permeated the atmosphere; from the stewardesses afraid because of the change in weight distribution as the herd of men ran to the back of the aircraft, and from the men because they were completely ignorant about the situation. I honestly thought we might not make it over the mountains, or at least the rear portion wouldn't, as fifty Afghan men were huddled at the back of the plane. I closed my eyes and kept praying. When I finally opened my eyes, I saw the mountains below us and knew we were safely airborne and on our way home. At that time, I thought to myself that I would never again return to this backward place. I did not understand that even at that moment God was preparing me to return to Afghanistan. God was readying me to have my world rocked and my perspective shattered.

Philippians 4:6-7
Be anxious for nothing, but in everything by prayer and supplication, with thanksgiving, let your requests be made known to God; and the peace of God, which surpasses all understanding, will guard your hearts and minds through Christ Jesus.

Letter 8 - First Day

As I write this, it's a bit past 4:00 a.m., and the call to prayer has begun. I just spent some time out on the third floor roof taking in

*the cool morning air and the beautiful lights of Kabul spread over
the hillside. It's so surreal to be here thinking that just 48 hours ago,
I was sleeping in my bed back home wondering what this first night
would be like. It took me a while to figure out how to write to you this
morning because when I signed on, everything on the internet page
was written in Arabic. I couldn't even figure out where to sign in,
forgetting that everything is written right to left. After several trials,
I finally found the right button. I had to laugh; not being able to read
Google wasn't something I had thought of.*

*We arrived about 1:00 p.m. yesterday afternoon. We landed at a
much improved airport, complete with a jet bridge and a transportation
bus that took us the quarter mile to where our contacts would be.
Customs and immigration went better than we could have imagined;
all of our luggage arrived without incident and was waiting for us as
we passed immigration. We were able to validate our visas right there,
saving us a trip and hours at the embassy later. We are now official
and legal for our first three months in Afghanistan.*

*After connecting with our host, we traveled by van to our new
temporary home. As we drove, I couldn't help but watch Hank and
Laney as they took everything in, trying to reconcile their expectations
with the new reality. Hank was so cute. He just kept looking out the
window and telling Laney, "This is going to be the best adventure
EVER!" Laney was a little quiet but soon warmed up to our host
family, telling them about our time in Dubai.*

*We are living on the third floor of a local guesthouse. We have two
rooms, a bathroom, and small common area. We also have a wonderful
rooftop patio right outside our bedrooms that overlooks the city. I
can already tell that this space will end up being a wonderful outside
retreat in the days to come. Yesterday was close to 90 degrees in the
afternoon, but it is dry here and doesn't feel that warm. This morning
when I went out, it had to be in the upper 50's, crisp and cool; it was
wonderful. As I sat overlooking the city and listening to the call to*

prayer over the city speakers, I was reminded that "Dorothy is not in Kansas anymore." Last night we had to teach the kids how to take a bucket bath and remind them not to use the water when they brushed their teeth. There were lessons on voltage and outlets and how to find the safe room (sealed room used when there are bombs or air raids). We wear slippers in the house and not shoes and always keep our chadar (scarf) by the door, as we have to wear it even on the roof.

The view from the rooftop is amazing! There has been a lot of reconstruction since I was here last; big buildings line the horizon and roads are paved that used to be impassible. In spite of the progress, there is much that is the same: broken buildings, soldiers with guns everywhere, people riding bikes and walking, open markets, chickens and goats crossing the roads, and lots of blue-cloaked women dotting the landscape. There are many reminders of how broken and war-torn this land is. This is a serious place, a place where people are preoccupied with survival, a place where it's not safe for the children to play outdoors, a place where it's not a child's right to attend school and learn a trade. We are humbled as we look at our new surroundings, humbled at what we have been given, the gifts of not only "stuff," but of liberty and truth, the gifts of imagination and dreams and goals, the gifts of education and support and kindness. The little things that we are allowed to participate in and enjoy on a daily basis, that most people here cannot even dream about, let alone ever experience.

Today we are going house hunting, a task that should be very interesting. My expectations of where and how I deserve to live have gone way down in the past months. Maybe I shouldn't say gone down; I should just say they have been adjusted. It's all relative, isn't it; what we deserve and what we are given? I'm excited to see what the city has to offer and see what surprises God has in store for us.

The children will start school on Saturday. Yes, I said Saturday. Friday is a holy day here so the children are all out of school on Thursdays and Fridays and they go to school on Saturdays and

Sundays. They are excited to get started, meet new friends, and be back in a classroom with others their age.

The sun is starting to come up now, and the house will be busy with meal preparation soon, so I best get my uncovered head upstairs and get dressed!

Have a good sleep everyone. We will keep watch for you until tomorrow!

Personal Reflections

Thinking back, I remember standing in the immigration line as I arrived in Afghanistan for the second time in my life, and how I couldn't help but notice how different things were from my first encounter. The area where we stood waiting for the immigration officer now had a hard tile floor instead of dirt. The windows had been replaced and the walls repaired and painted. There were even a few women standing in line with us, though no children other than our two. The structure of the airport had definitely improved. As our family waited in line, I was keenly aware of the uncomfortable stares from the men in the room. Though our heads were covered, and we were wearing completely Muslim-appropriate clothing, there was still no doubt that my daughter and I were foreigners. As we answered the immigration officer's questions, the low rumble of the voices in the background likely included conversations about why we were in their country. Driving out of the airport that day, I remember the stark contrast with my home country and how it nearly sucked the breath from my lungs. At every turn, there were Afghan soldiers carrying machine guns mixed in with the buyers and sellers along the side of the road. Struggling through the traffic was like navigating through a maze—stopping, turning, and winding in and out of crevices and small side roads trying to avoid the gridlock of the main streets. Halfway home, our driver decided to take a dirt path over the mountains, hoping to shorten our trip. As we were winding up the mountains, my view consisted not only of the city below me but of the small shoeless children walking up and down the steep terrain carrying plastic bottles and barrels full of water to their mountainside homes.

Some of the children I saw couldn't have been more than four or five years old. I wondered how many times each day they had to make that trip and if they ever had time to play and enjoy the beautiful fall weather. As far as I could see was city and dirt, not a patch of green anywhere. Donkeys attached to carts carrying goods up the mountain face as well as herds of fat bottom sheep lined the road. It was like stepping back in time. Most of the houses scattered upon the mountainside had no glass in their windows and their owners used old blankets and sheets to provide privacy from onlookers like me. It was evident that at one time some of the houses were quite beautiful and must have had running water and electricity as well as beautiful lush gardens. Now, however, the homes were just shells of their former glory and were barely standing, providing little shelter from the harsh winters and brutal summers of this desert land.

Just over the top of the mountain was the largest cemetery in the city. As far as the eye can see are flat rock headstones and green, black, and red flags. Green is the color of Islam, so every grave is decorated with something in green. There are no names or markers on the headstones, just positional differences indicating whether the person was a man or woman. If the headstone is facing the grave, like those common in the West, it is a man. If the headstone is turned at a ninety-degree angle, it is for a woman. The headstone placement is another example of the discrimination of women in this land. In the center of the cemetery is a large mosque with a blue dome roof; it is the focal point of this field of stone and dirt. During the Afghan New Year, the city gathers at this mosque to fly colorful kites and celebrate in hope of better days. The contrast of seeing so many men, women, and children crowded into this area, laughing and flying kites of beautiful colors, dotting the skyline like balloons while their dead family members lay beneath their feet, is profound.

My first impressions of Afghanistan would prove to be some of my most treasured. As the weeks and months wore on, we often forgot about those first sights and sounds. Our surroundings became familiar and sometimes oppressive. We got caught up in the "ugliness" of the country and forgot about its beauty. I remember seeing the mountains for the first time without snow on them. The only other time I had visited Afghanistan was in the winter, and everything was white. In our late summer arrival, everything looked completely different; it had a new kind of beauty to it. The mountains were rugged and majestic, full of a harsh and unforgiving quality, a beauty unlike anything I had seen. The few trees that were there were green with leaves and the roses were in full bloom.

I loved that Afghanistan was ten hours ahead of our home time and that we got to live out each day before all our family and friends back home. It was a weird fun thing to have a head start on the happenings in the world. I was given the privilege of praying for my children and friends and family before they opened their eyes, praying for the things that lay ahead of them. I saw the moon rise and sun set before everyone else, and yet it was the same moon and sun for us all. When I was feeling lonely, I would go out on my rooftop and look at the moon, sometimes seeming so close that I could touch it. I would look up and think, "This is the same moon that my children back home will see during their night." It was comforting and made me feel not so far away. I often wished that they could see what I saw, experience what I did. I wondered if they would love Afghanistan the way I did and for the same reasons or if they would find it ugly and difficult. I was glad that God was God to us all, no matter where we were.

Standing on my rooftop, I could see in a complete circle around me. From the front I could see four mosques, two main traffic routes, many roadside shops, a wedding hall, and a soccer field, buzzing with life all hours of the day and night. From behind, I had a fantastic view of the trellised houses scattered up and down the mountainside. I could watch the daily routine of life as it unfolded each day. Some days I would stand on my rooftop and pray for the city. I would pray against the dark cloud of evil that suffocated and paralyzed its people. I would pray against the lack of education and against the devices of the enemy that sought to steal from, kill, and destroy the people of this nation. I would pray that the light of truth would permeate and penetrate the closed minds of its leaders. I would pray that God would provide a way for these people to find health and education and peace.

Afghanistan is a strange mix of desert and mountains, rugged and vast, intimidating and beautiful. There are snow-capped mountains and valleys of green, life-giving streams flowing into crystal clear pools, and sometimes hardly a tree in sight. These contrasts have a harsh, rugged yet beautiful allure to them. They reminded me of the Psalms of David and the terrain our forefathers must have known.

Some of the mountain peaks surrounding Kabul are covered with snow nearly year round and their vastness both protects and isolates the people of the city from the outside world. Many times, as I would stand on my rooftop and gaze across the city, I would catch myself becoming lost in its beauty and easily forgetting that any kind of world existed beyond its horizon. How can there be wars and famines, financial gain and ruin, sports games and reality TV, earthquakes and tsunamis, royal weddings and movie premiers all happening while I stand in the quiet beauty of these mountains? From that rooftop, I watched many sunsets and sunrises while listening to the backdrop chants of the Muslim call to prayer. In some ways, life here has existed unchanged generation after generation with the people knowing little of the advances and provisions of the modern world—each and every one of their days remaining the same.

As I would gaze out over the rugged beauty, I was always reminded of how big our God is and how much He loves each and every one of us. It is sometimes difficult to acknowledge how easily we can have an attitude of superiority toward those less fortunate than ourselves. Because we are more educated, have greater provision, and live in the free world, we can feel that somehow we are better. But God created us ALL in His image and sent His Son so that ALL may live and be reconciled to their Creator. I know with certainty that there are people in Afghanistan whose intelligence far exceeds anyone I have ever met, yet they lack the opportunity to exercise it to its full potential. Regardless of the image we may have of the people of this misunderstood nation, we are no better than they in the sight of God. It is only by the grace of God we were born into the place where we live and have what we have. I believe the reason the United States has been considered the greatest country in the world is because many of our forefathers sacrificed everything they had to build our nation on Godly principles. America was established on the truth of the Word of God. What does our Constitution say? All people are created equal.

Isaiah 43:19
*Behold, I will do a new thing, now it shall spring
forth; shall you not know it? I will even make a road
in the wilderness and rivers in the desert.*

Letter 9 - A New Normal

Okay everyone, if you are just sitting down to read, you might want to go get a cup of coffee and settle in, because this letter will be a long one.

I can't believe we have been here almost a week; I swear it's really been a month. So much has happened each day and with such a huge learning curve, it seems that each day is really a week in itself. Since the last time I wrote, we have looked at half a dozen houses, been to multiple markets, met dozens of people, and started the kids in school.

Their first day of school was Saturday, so while you were going to soccer games or mowing your yards, we were navigating through a brand new world of education on the other side of the world. The first day at pick-up, I was reminded that we were not on familiar ground when, as I waited for our kids to come out of the building, there were armed guards with machine guns and full bulletproof gear waiting for the children of their employers. I was also only one of two moms there waiting, as in this culture the men and the hired help pick up children from school.

Each morning we must pass though an armed security gate with large barricades and long candy-striped poles, each manned by an Afghan guard with a machine gun. Every car is checked underneath with a large mirror on a long handle to look for any explosives, and all doors and the trunk are opened for inspection as well. Once inside the gate, the school is much like small public schools anywhere. The kids all speak English and are taught an international curriculum; they spend their days in classrooms studying the basics along with computer, art, music, and PE. The Dari language class sets it apart a bit, I guess. Hank has been studying writing right to left and copying the characters of Dari over and over. Today we learned how to say the days of the week and basic greetings. Yesterday Laney and I went to an open house for the local ballet class where she will be taking a ballet and tap class, and I will be taking an adult lyrical dance class. We are excited for classes to begin next week when we will be able to meet more people from the community. The ballet class is in a studio that is completely off limits to men, so it's one of the only places we can all be together with our heads uncovered and participate in something creative and beautiful put to music, something that was banned for years when the former government was in power.

Yesterday William and I ventured out to the "mall" so we could buy cell phones. The mall is located downtown and is part of a five-star hotel. The seven-floor structure houses the only working escalator in the whole country. The stores are filled with some of the most expensive items anywhere—electronics, jewels, and designer clothes, both Western and native. As we entered the building, we had to be searched and go through a metal detector. There are some bargains at the mall though. If we go to the "movie" store, we can purchase almost any movie imaginable—even ones not released yet— for only $2.

The mall trip was a bit of a contrast from the day before when I went to the local market to buy food supplies for the kids' lunches. To get to the local market, I had to sit in traffic as we waited for herds of goats and sheep to cross the road. After driving on both sides of the road and dodging large holes and donkey-pulled carts filled with everything from spinach to furniture, we arrived at the market. Now, please understand, this is not a quaint little craft and art market; this is an area about the size of two football fields filled with little shacks and metal moving containers converted into stores housing everything imaginable. Entering the large bazaar, we passed through the meat market. This was not a store with open freezers of wrapped meat or even a meat counter with a butcher; this meat market has whole cow, sheep, and goat carcasses hanging in the open and we had to walk past them. The carcasses are all without their heads and skin (the heads are proudly displayed separately for purchase). At this point, it's really helpful that I am covering my head with a scarf because I can use it to cover my nose and my eyes if the flies get too bad. After passing through the meat market, we entered the food section. In this area, we can dig through large barrels of individual cereal boxes or buy MREs (meals-ready-to-eat) that have come from the military bases. If we are lucky, we find Gatorade and Cliff bars. The foreign community here is very grateful for the international military for many reasons, but one big one is the availability of Western comfort food. As the food on base nears expiration, it is sold or given to the local shopkeepers (or stolen), creating a large foreign shopping heaven! The "market" is so diverse that across from the shopkeeper that sells dates and cardamom, you can buy body-building protein powder.

After leaving the food section, the next area is clothes and bedding, with row after row of military boots, fatigues, and vests along with the occasional "American Eagle" jeans and polo shirts. In the bedding section are sheets, blankets, comforters, and towels... just imagine the largest garage sale ever and double it! In this market, instead of baskets to push purchased items to the car, are wheelbarrows complete with hired help to push them, we simply stop at the desired shop, make the purchase, and the "helper" will push the treasures to our vehicle. If shoppers have come in a taxi and the things won't fit in the "boot" (trunk), the helper will simply tie the things to the roof of the car (for a small fee, of course). It's one-stop shopping, not quite Wal-Mart or Target, but much more entertaining; except I'm not sure who is more entertained: me the shopper, or all the people staring at me because I am a foreign woman shopping there.

We have spent two full days shopping for housing; I am frustrated, confused, and overwhelmed. I have seen houses from one end of the spectrum to the other. Because we do not have a car and the kids and I will be at school each day, we really need something within walking distance of the school compound. I'm really trying not to have too high standards when looking at these places; but good grief, I don't really think I can "camp" all winter either. Some of the houses we have looked at would need a complete overhaul... anyone remember watching "Green Acres" as a kid? Well, that's about what some of these places look like. In addition to the list of things a house should have (i.e., water, toilet, kitchen, etc.), we also have to consider security and a place small enough to heat with a buxari (wood- or kerosene-burning stove). With security issues, it's necessary to have a ten-foot wall around the property with an iron gate. Inside the gate we need a chowkidar (guard) who lives in the corner of the property and keeps watch over things 24 hours a day. It may be necessary to have barbed wire strung on top of the wall. It's good to pick a house that is in a well-secured area; for instance, an area where important officials or large businesses have compounds, because they have 24-hour armed guards. Some would argue, though, that it's not the best choice to live by these officials, as we could become a target for anyone who doesn't like them. Many of the houses are multiple family houses, as most cultures don't have a problem with sharing living spaces. We did find a very nice two-year-old house that is ready to move into, but it is a multi-family house. It does have two separate entrances though and is very close to the school. We are now in search of another family that might want to make the jump with us into the housing craziness and the "psycho-landlords." There are so many things to consider when finding a house that we were constantly re-prioritizing, swapping one thing for another. Once we find a house, of course, I have to start the whole learning curve of how to shop and cook along with portable hot water heaters, purifying water, and staying warm in a country without any consistently safe form of heating. The whole thing is just a bit much right now.

Tomorrow we start a two-day orientation and security briefing: two days of lectures on the history of the country, language, cooking, housing, and the basics of living in this crazy place. Hopefully I'll feel more empowered to tackle all these new challenges. I know that things will get better; it's all just so foreign and new. Things that we do all the time at home without a second thought take so much concentrated effort right now. I am looking forward to the time when I can just live, and it all feels "normal," when everything I am doing doesn't take conscious thought. My sister and I always tell each other when new "seasons" occur in our lives that we just have to learn to live a "new normal." What was comfortable and routine before is replaced with new and unfamiliar; but with time, it too will settle into a routine that becomes effortless. For now I am putting one foot in front of the other and pushing forward looking for those roses in my dust. The other day when looking at one of the houses, I was admiring a beautiful pink rose bush that was in the front courtyard of the property. As I was getting ready to leave, the chowkidar (guard) came over and cut four beautiful roses, one for each of us; it was a reminder of the beauty in the small things of this adventure. As you finish reading this letter, sit back and think of a "rose" in your life, something that truly brings beauty to you in the midst of your crazy, wonderful life.

Personal Reflection

New seasons of life are unnerving and scary. The most mundane of tasks can seem overwhelming and impossible. It's comforting to know, though, that it is just a season; time marches on and things become familiar and routine after a time. Things that seemed impossible can be done effortlessly and with confidence, but it takes time and patience. Those who have given birth know what finding a "new normal" is like. The first few weeks are a blur not knowing how to function each day. I wondered if I'd ever feel "normal" again and if I would be able to navigate through life with this new little person. After about six weeks, a time came when I stopped and realized that I was doing life without consciously thinking about every step. I was empowered by the realization that though life looks different, I was thriving, not just surviving. I was actually moving forward, not just treading water. Every new season brings adjustment and challenges; but with the Lord's grace and help, it doesn't take long until the "new normal" is found.

I never expected that there would be a time in my life that I would be navigating the details of life in a country at war, where everything was totally different, including my own identity and purpose. Living in Afghanistan was never the "new normal" I expected and yet it was no surprise to God. He knew before I was born that I would be thrust into a situation that involved safe rooms, machine guns, escape routes, and security check points. I am so grateful that I learned that although the new seasons in life can unnerve me and take me by surprise, they are never a surprise to God. He sees the big picture as well as all of the small details. I learned about this when looking through a beautiful kaleidoscope a dear friend sent with me to Afghanistan. It was something I enjoyed greatly, and often when life got a little crazy and I found myself overwhelmed, I took it out and would sit and look through the prism, letting the colored pieces fall into organized shapes of beauty. Each turn would create a unique, amazing picture never to be duplicated. I would be reminded that each new season of my life was like the process of turning the kaleidoscope. Though it simply contained hundreds of little broken pieces of glass, when held up to the light and turned gently, the broken pieces would fall into place, creating a beautiful work of art. In the same way, when we look at our lives, filled with various pieces and colors and hold them up to the Son, we can clearly see the work of art that each season of life really is.

Whatever season you find yourself in today, I challenge you to hold the pieces of your hours, days, weeks and months up to the Light and let the Lord show you a glimpse of the masterpiece that He is creating you to be.

Philippians 3:13-14
Brethren, I do not count myself to have apprehended; but one thing I do, forgetting those things which are behind and reaching forward to those things which are ahead, I press toward the goal for the prize of the upward call of God in Christ Jesus.

Letter 10 - A Life of Contrast

As I sit down to write this letter, I am completely overwhelmed at the amount of information that I want to relate to you. Each day I am bombarded with so many sights and sounds and emotions that it seems that one day is a week of experiences. Every time we drive out of our compound is a new adventure in itself.

I think the best way to communicate some of these things is to relate to you the contrasts of my life back home to my life here.

• *At home, I lived in a house with 13 rooms on 2 1/2 acres of land on which to roam; here I live in three rooms with a compilation of less than 700 square feet, a space that is within a home in which another couple live. The house is surrounded with ten-foot walls with a locked gate and a full-time security guard.*

• *At home, I drive my own car, do my own shopping, and go about my day often completely alone; here I cannot drive and have to always sit in the back seat of a vehicle; I cannot ride alone in a car without my husband or another male family member; I can never go anywhere alone and must always have a man with me when I do my shopping.*

• *Back home, I can wear sleeveless shirts and shorts; here I must have my arms and legs covered and never leave my house without a headscarf. Even when I go onto the roof to collect our laundry, I must wear a scarf, as the neighbors may see me from their roofs. I also must keep my backside covered all the time, so I most often need to wear an abaya, or overcoat, over my skirt or pants when outside of my home.*

• *Back home, I can talk to anyone I wish and start a conversation about any topic I please; here I should not talk to anyone unless it's absolutely necessary and I should never ever blow my nose in public or laugh out loud outside of my house.*

• *Back home, the traffic always flows in an orderly fashion driving only on the right side of the road and always following road signs and signals; here, the traffic is allowed to flow anywhere it wishes and the police sit in their cars and yell instructions to the drivers about when and where to turn.*

Some other interesting contrasts -

You know you are not in America when:

- *Sheep and goats cross the busy roads regularly being led by a donkey and cart.*
- *You can buy meat hanging from big hooks without any refrigeration.*
- *You can buy MREs (meals ready-to-eat) and military boots and fatigues in the local market.*
- *You have to wear pants under your skirt even if it touches the ground.*
- *There are guards carrying machine guns and checking taxis for explosives at your child's school.*
- *You can't tell the difference between fireworks and gunfire.*
- *It's cold enough in your house that you can leave your milk out overnight without worrying it will spoil.*
- *You have to take anything you need dry cleaned to Dubai.*
- *It's okay to wear florals with stripes and you actually think it might be cute.*
- *A family outing is a walk to the end of your street to buy bananas.*
- *You have to put your coat on in the middle of the night to go to the bathroom.*
- *An extra room is also the extra refrigerator.*
- *You are given a security briefing every day before leaving for school.*
- *The electricity goes out several times a day, and no one even notices.*
- *Straight leg jeans are not considered fashionable but immodest.*
- *The whole family gets excited because you found cheese in the market.*
- *An open pickup truck carrying men with machine guns is a daily occurrence on the roads.*

- *You watch the clock impatiently for 9:00 p.m. (a decent hour to go to bed).*
- *Your first thought when visiting a five star hotel is, "Wow, nice grass."*
- *Your household celebrates when a new restaurant makes the approved security list.*
- *You dust your house and two hours later it looks like you have been gone a month.*
- *You pass a man on the side of the road painting the rear ends of his sheep pink.*
- *The shopkeeper has to dust off the top of your soda can before handing it to you.*
- *Your conversations around the table consist of talking about the extra value meals at McDonald's.*
- *You see a one-legged man riding a bicycle.*
- *Your driver drives your car on the sidewalk, and everyone thinks it's normal.*
- *A minivan for a family is actually a motorcycle.*
- *You have to carry your own toilet paper and passport everywhere you go.*
- *You see someone going to the bathroom on the side of the road while talking on a cell phone.*
- *The neighbor's rooster is more reliable than your alarm clock.*

Okay, I think you get the point. I spend a lot of energy each day coming to grips with the contrasts in my life right now; I am very busy creating a "new normal" for my family and myself.

Though the contrast is great and the emotional toll is heavy at times, we are so grateful for the provisions and blessings in our lives. On Friday, our family attended the memorial service for the ten team members killed here last month. The entire expatriate community came together to honor those slain. We heard story after story of the remarkable lives of these men and women: lives of love and honor that they lived for the people of this country, their commitment to live and work here in order that others may benefit. The experience was both humbling and challenging; it caused us to reflect on the important things of life, the moments, days and weeks that we have that are opportunities to live bigger than ourselves. The one theme that kept being expressed was that every team member who had lost his or her life would have gladly given it up over and over again for the causes he or she believed in and the beautiful people of this country. The "contrast" of life is not so difficult to contend with when one's perspective is adjusted by an event like this.

Life is fragile and short. Let's determine to live with conviction and purpose, to follow after the things we are passionate about—our faith, our family, our friends, and those around us who live in the darkness of hopelessness.

Personal Reflection

As humans, we complicate life by picking apart and analyzing its events. We want to understand everything there is to know about things and work tirelessly to control them. The bottom line is: we can't control life. We don't control when it begins or when it ends; we think we can, but only God has that power. All we can do is try to live each day with as much conviction of truth as we can. Life is short and we have no guarantees. We don't know the number of days we are given or how much time we have to accomplish what God has asked us to do. We must live with a determined purpose to have no regrets and live each moment as if it were our last. We want to know that our lives have counted for something, that we have lived bigger than ourselves and that there was purpose in our lives as well as our deaths. We can only accomplish this if we are determined to do so. I am challenged by the lives of the team members who died. The example of their lives and deaths stirs me to be more determined than ever to live life with the goal of fulfilling the purpose God has assigned me.

During the months we lived in Afghanistan, the "Nuristan team," the ten who had died, would play a big part in all of our lives. We became friends with some of the friends and family members of the slain team and would walk out the grieving process with them. We were honored to attend the memorial service for the team only days after arriving in the country, a service over three hundred people attended to celebrate the lives of those brave men and women. The beautifully colored threads of those team members' lives were intricately woven into the tapestry of life in Kabul and, like a beautiful Afghan carpet, each member's distinctive color brought beauty to the whole. Both Afghans and expatriates of the community were richer for knowing the members of that team who selflessly sacrificed their all for the Afghan people. Their deaths were not in vain and God will use the testimony of their lives to impact others over and over again. These martyrs have a special place in heaven, but they also have a special place in our hearts and in the hearts of many Afghans. What satan meant for evil, God most certainly used and is using for good (John 15:12-13).

Letter 11 - Today is a Hard Day

Today is a hard day. I am battling a lot of feelings and really have no place to sort them out; so the result…another letter.

Today, as I took the kids to school and left our van and driver outside the security gate to walk with the kids to the drop-off point, I again was reminded of how different my life is now. When I came back out of the gate, I realized that my van had left me…a result of a cross-cultural miscommunication. Now, waiting for a ride most places is not usually a big deal, but here it's a different story. I, as a foreigner, had to wait behind the security line, a line of soldiers with machine guns. As a woman, I can't engage in conversation and shouldn't even make eye contact with those around me. I was frustrated and mad, not because I had been left, but because my liberties had been taken away, partly because of the security situation, but mostly because of the "culture" of this place. I know it must be even harder for the older women here, when they have had liberty and then had it removed; maybe less difficult for those who have known nothing else. I know what it's like to have had certain independences and a voice of public expression, both things I took for granted a great deal before coming here. These two gifts are such a part of our individuality; they help make up who we are and how we are known. Coming and going independently and having freedom of expression in our conversations helps define how we feel about ourselves and how we feel about others. These expressions help us define how we fit in social settings. As these gifts have been altered in my life, I am forced to re-evaluate that process. Am I still the same person God created me to be, even if I cannot always outwardly express it? Is the gift of individuality still a gift if I am isolated all the time? It takes a lot of self-searching and dialogue to be comfortable in my own skin, alone with myself and God.

The experience I had today magnifies another way that I am different from the women who live here. Women's voices of expression here are not completely lost, as they do have a very strong social network among themselves, behind closed doors but within a large network of women who live together. The dynamics are greatly altered by the way the nationals here live a life of community. Our Western style of living independently, separated by houses and sometimes great distances from our family, makes our need for expression much more difficult to get met. Though there are other expatriate women living here, we are separated by houses and distance that cannot easily be bridged. And though we come from a good understanding of Western thinking, we are strangers, not bound by family ties and years of living together. When we come together, the fellowship is sweet but shallow, simply because of our "distance" from one another. Don't get me wrong; I am so grateful for the expatriate community here and the connection and bond of these families that is essential to our survival here. The community has been very welcoming and supportive since our arrival. However, the community here, though strong, is also diverse; there are many nationalities represented; language and experiences all play a significant role in the ability to "bond."

I felt this in a very tangible way yesterday when I started a ballet class for adults taught at the school. I was excited to begin, not only for the exercise and opportunity to get out of the house, but also for the sense of community and friendship I hoped to discover. When I arrived at the class, I quickly realized that although we were all women living in a difficult country together, we were vastly diverse in our languages, cultures, and experiences. Some of the women are young, just out of college, here teaching school. They live together, eating all their meals together and never leaving the compound. Even within that group, there are probably four or five different nationalities and languages represented. The other women are a diverse group—some single, some married, some with children, some without, some who have lived here for years even through the Taliban rule, and others have been here just a short time. Within this group, several nationalities and languages are represented. In this mixed group, I found myself feeling as isolated as I do alone in my little apartment. I know that with time this will change as we experience the same things together and learn of each other; the sense of community will develop. The national women here in this "closed" culture do not often have these feelings of isolation because they have grown up with their community – moms, aunts, and sisters – by their sides. They have little need for outside social contact because their sense of community and identity is met within the walls of their homes. Now I know we could debate the validity of both sides of this coin, and I'm not presenting it to argue the pros and cons of each. I am just expressing the difficulty of adjusting to the different cultural norms. Maybe another day I'll take on the pros and cons of each side of things, because both contain some very valid aspects.

I had two other experiences this week dealing with the lack of independence and personal voice. Saturday, as we got ready to leave for school, our driver had not arrived yet, and it became apparent that we would need to make other arrangements. At the last minute, we decided that we would need to take a taxi. In this culture, taking a taxi, especially for a short distance, is very normal and easy if you're a man. For me, the story is a bit different. I had to ask one of the male employees here to travel with me, not only because he speaks the language and would make sure that as a foreigner I would get a "good" price; but because I cannot ride in a car with a man I don't know and certainly cannot have conversation or interaction with him. It's a bit humbling to have someone do all the talking and bidding for you.

On another day, my husband and I and our housemates went to the local market to get supplies. As the four of us entered the market, the women got separated from the men. While we were waiting for the guys to catch up, a group of young men approached us. As they passed by, one of the boys reached out and grabbed me inappropriately. I was so shocked; I didn't know what to do. Now, in this culture it's completely acceptable for things like that to happen; maybe I shouldn't say "acceptable"—that's not really fair. However, it's very common, and it's not acceptable for a woman to protest. I felt completely helpless. At home, no one would have the nerve to do something like that and think they wouldn't be confronted and even disciplined for it. Once again, I felt the pains of isolation and loss of voice and independence. I also realized how vulnerable and at risk I was as a woman. I really need the help and protection of my husband not just to survive here, but to thrive. Though it may sound contradictory to the things I have expressed, in this culture I really like the fact that I can depend on the strength and protection of my spouse; I need him to function here. As a Westerner, this may be hard to admit; but perhaps we should be more comfortable with letting our husbands take on this kind of role, even in our own culture...but that's another letter.

Well, I know this ended up getting long, but thank you for letting me vent and process. I do feel better.

Personal Reflections

Having my levels of independence adjusted for me while living in a Muslim culture was challenging and lonely at times. Though difficult, it taught me to reflect on what true freedom is. I found out that freedom is something experienced, not only in our physical world, but in our hearts. When we know and understand the work of Jesus Christ in our lives, we can truly experience freedom. It doesn't' matter if I am allowed to drive a car, speak in public, shop independently—those things do not define my freedom. The liberty I have from sin and the relationship I have with Jesus defines my freedom. It is not easy to live with so many physical and social restrictions - certainly not; but I am not defined by those things. I am defined by what I possess in my inner self, what Christ gives and takes away from me, taking my sins and replacing them with forgiveness, taking my pride and expectations and replacing them with knowledge of Him and His plans and purposes, giving me an understanding of why He made me. I don't need to "do" anything to be free; I just need to be and let God be in me; that is freedom!

When I arrived in Afghanistan, I became acutely aware that all the freedoms of my home country had disappeared the moment I passed through the immigration line. It was like a coat I hung on a hook at the door of the country and was not allowed to put back on until stepping on that plane again to return home. It is hard to describe what it's like to have known nothing but total freedom only to lose that freedom in a moment. Really, "lose" is not a good word; in reality, I gave it away. I chose to leave my country of freedoms and enter a world of restrictions; it was completely my choice. Realizing this made me even more aware of the differences between me and my "sisters" in Afghanistan. For the women of Afghanistan, restrictions are not a choice; they are mandated. These boundaries are thrust upon each beautiful woman at birth. Most of these precious women have never known any other way. Some, however, are keenly aware of the contrasts but have no way of experiencing anything different

I asked the Lord what He wanted me to do while on this journey. My husband had a specific role to play, but the details of my "job description" were unclear. Living in a Muslim country, I knew that my daily life would look very different than it did back home. I knew that I would have little opportunity for independent interactions with the local people and few opportunities to work at a specific task. The Lord gently reminded me of His request of me after returning from Afghanistan the first time. He had told me to use the stories and experiences of my life to simply be a voice for those who have none, to represent a people who cannot represent themselves.

After recalling His words, I continued to be compelled to write and document our experiences and thoughts and feelings in order to share what I was learning and translate my life lessons and personal revelations to others. Hopefully it will help others to understand life in Afghanistan and the people living there, to compel them to pray for this broken land.

Galatians 3:26-29

For you are all sons of God through faith in Christ Jesus.
For as many of you as were baptized into Christ have put
on Christ. There is neither Jew nor Greek, there is neither
slave nor free, there is neither male nor female; for you are
all one in Christ Jesus. And if you are Christ's, then you
are Abraham's seed, and heirs according to the promise.

Letter 12 - I Just Want to Make Granola!

I just want to make granola! In my desire to find a "new normal," I
decided a few days ago that I would make some homemade granola.

William has to leave very early in the mornings before we get breakfast ready. He loves homemade granola, so I thought it would be fun to make a batch for him. I thought granola wouldn't be so hard—oats, nuts, fruit, right? Oh well, think again. I thought of doing this project three days ago and that's how long it's taken me to even get started. Two days ago I went to the market and got half a kilo of currants and some dried apricots, almonds, and even found a can of mixed nuts from the military base. It then took another two days to find flour, brown sugar, oil, oats, and butter. Okay, I have my ingredients...not ready yet. Now I have to filter water to wash the dried fruits and then soak them in filtered water overnight to soften them. So this morning I got up all excited that today would be the day I would attempt to finish the project. I put the ingredients into a bowl and got ready to spread them on the cookie sheet to bake; not so hard, right? Think again! After half an hour and two boxes of matches, I couldn't get my gas stove to light; the burners will ignite but not the oven! Now for those of you who may have a gas stove, you may be asking, "Why doesn't it just light itself?" Well, that would happen at home; but this is not home, and I have a kitchen that was constructed in a bathroom. The stove we have has a separate gas can that attaches to the stove somewhat like an outdoor gas grill. I have to turn the gas on, then light a match and hope that the gas is flowing enough to catch in the stove; obviously that simple step had a breakdown somewhere! Okay, I'll just wait until Will gets home.

After all the preparations, I now need to clean up. I'll just put the dishes in the dishwasher and start it while I go on to something else. Oh wait, I'm in Kabul - there are no dishwashers! I have to heat a kettle of hot water, fill my sink with cold water and add the boiling water, wash all my dishes, drain the water, then boil more hot water so I can then rinse them. I have to lay them all out to dry so that the unfiltered water on the dishes evaporates. After an hour or so, I can finally put the dishes away just in time to start more food preparation and do the whole process again.

Honestly, I was feeling pretty sorry for myself until I looked out the window into my neighbor's yard where I saw my neighbors sitting on the ground with a kettle of hot water pouring it over a basin where she was washing her clothes by hand while also taking care of her two-year-old! Next to her is a big pot on an open fire where she is preparing some kind of food for their lunch... after lunch she will boil water and wash her dishes right there on the porch. Okay, I have it pretty good. Frustrated? YES. Anything to complain about? ABSOLUTELY NOT!

I STILL JUST WANT TO MAKE GRANOLA!

Personal Reflection

Life can get pretty frustrating when our expectations get in the way of living life. We wake each day with a plan in our heads. Let's be honest. We are all control freaks. We all want to know what lies ahead and to do whatever we can to manipulate life so that we can have the outcomes we want. We don't see the big picture in life; only God does. He is trying to get us to move to the left or the right so that His plans can be accomplished, but we want to know what's up. We want to call the shots. Learning to let God direct our lives can be a challenging and painful thing. Giving up control can be unnerving and scary unless we know to Whom we are giving up that control.

If we understand God's character, if we really know that He is good and perfect and that He only wants what is good and perfect for us, then why is it so hard to hand life over to Him? We have to make a conscious decision that either God is who He says He is, or He is not. Either God can control our lives and produce good in us, or He needs our help to do it.

When we get our flesh involved in the mix of life, there is little room for anything but frustration and conflict. Even if the things we are trying to do are good, if they are not God's, they will end up sucking the life right out of us. We have to be willing to turn our expectations over to God each and every day, ask Him to direct our lives, and let Him orchestrate the details. It's not easy for us control freaks, but there is great reward and peace in the journey when we are willing.

John 15:16

You did not choose Me, but I chose you and appointed you that you should go and bear fruit, and that your fruit should remain, that whatever you ask the Father in My name He may give you.

CHAPTER 5 – Simple Treasures

Matthew 6:19-21

Do not lay up for yourselves treasures on earth, where moth and rust destroy and where thieves break in and steal; but lay up for yourselves treasures in heaven, where neither moth nor rust destroys and where thieves do not break in and steal. For where your treasure is, there your heart will be also.

Letter 13 - Putting Down Roots

Well, I think we are here to stay. We just finished our second full week here and it doesn't seem possible. Haven't we actually been gone two months? I know I have navigated through way more than two weeks of experiences for sure.

A week ago today we made the decision on our housing. After looking for about a week at lots of different properties and options, never feeling peace about any of them, we decided to do some renovating and turn the third floor area we have been renting here into a little apartment. We went and picked up our furniture that was so graciously being kept in a friend's yard and brought it to the house. We turned the small dressing room off the bathroom into a kitchen, moving our stove and refrigerator up, putting a shelf onto the countertop for supplies and moving the water purifier into the last bit of space in the corner where it fit perfectly. There is a small sink that was broken, so we had a plumber come and check it out; and we discovered that the drain was just plugged—a quick and simple fix. Our bedroom is quite large, so we were able to move our couch and two sitting chairs along with a coffee table and two end tables into the room along with a queen bed and large desk. We divided the room into two parts, one half the living room and one half the bedroom. Across the landing that has a beautiful large window overlooking the mountains is the kids' room where they each have a desk, a bed, and a dresser. Our new little home is warm and cozy and full of wonderful sunshine.

I won't go into all the reasons why we didn't have peace about the properties we looked at; but I will tell you that without a shadow of doubt, we are where we are supposed to be. We have privacy and independence along with the company of a wonderful couple who live downstairs with whom we can share our lives here. When winter comes, we will be able to share the responsibility of burning the wood in buxaries (indoor heaters); buying, gathering, hauling and burning our wood to stay warm. Also, with two women in the house, we are able to share the responsibility of shopping and meals, something neither of us can do on our own. It's not necessarily a Western arrangement, but it's perfect for this difficult place. We are grateful for the warm and peaceful house shared with wonderful friends.

An added bonus of our little apartment is that, being on the third floor, we have access to the roof, where we have a panoramic view of the city and the mountains, a peaceful place to spend time.

Now, after sharing where we ended up, I have to tell you about an incident that was very humbling for me yesterday. We went to help a young couple and their three children, ages three, two, and nine months, clean a house they just rented. This couple has been trying to get back into Afghanistan for five months, and they were living in one small room in Dubai while they waited for their visas. They arrived this past Sunday, and they were thrilled to find a house on Wednesday. When we arrived at the property to help them, I recognized that the house was the first house we had looked at when arriving here. The place was a mess and needed so much work that we didn't even consider it. Now I was back in that same house, which was basically in the same shape as it was when we saw it, except for a fresh coat of paint. We spent the next several hours scrubbing paint off windows and wood frames and washing off layers of dirt that I swear were one half inch thick. The kitchen was the worst. Several times I gagged as I washed and scrubbed and scraped stuff loose with a pocketknife.

I felt such sadness for this couple that several times I was completely overwhelmed. After finishing, the couple wanted to have us stay for some snacks to dedicate the home and express gratitude for our help. As this young mother began to tell her story about how much they love the people of this country and how they have given up so much to be here, my heart was pierced. They went on to tell us that in the past four years of being in this country, they have been forced by

landlords to move ten times. Now I don't know about you, but that
thought alone is enough to send me over the edge, especially in this
place where everything is ten times more difficult. As I sat on the
floor and shared a coke with these precious people, I was ashamed of
how prideful I had been as I looked at the same property that these
sweet people were calling home. I had thought myself to be too good
for this place, saying it wouldn't be responsible to take my children
into a house like that. These people were brought to tears of joy that
God had provided for them and that they now had a place where their
children could play and move about.

The feelings this experience surfaced in me were intense and
shameful and at the same time a wonderful reminder that in life we
have to be so careful that our flesh does not get in the way of what
we are to learn along the way. I am so grateful for God's goodness
in my life; and at the same time, I take so many things for granted.
EVERTHING that is good in our lives, starting with our very breath,
is a gift; a gift that is undeserved and unmerited, but given by grace
and love.

Personal Reflection

Pride is an ugly thing that controls and manipulates us.
Our flesh is so easily swayed to believe that we deserve so
much in life. In reality, the only thing any of us deserves is
hell. Everything above hell is a gift from God. The sacrifice
made by God provided us with the gift of life and eternal
relationship with our Creator. Everything on this earth and the
world to come are gifts from that sacrifice. It's a hard reality,
but I believe it is the truth; and unless we can reconcile that
truth in our hearts, we will be forever so full of ourselves that
we cannot see the gifts in front of us!

Our living arrangements while in Afghanistan ended up
being one of the greatest and most profound gifts we received.
We had no way of understanding what was ahead of us for

that year, no way to know what would be best. We prayed and walked forward making decisions out of our experience and what seemed right. God had different plans for us than we did, and He knew exactly what was needed personally and corporately for our time there.

Reflecting on our time in Afghanistan, I honestly don't know if we could have survived in any other arrangement. Maybe "survive" is not a good word, but I certainly know we would not have thrived and been able to do what we needed to do. God knew and walked us down a road that, at times, was confusing; but nevertheless right. And when we stood at the crossroads of decisions, we knew without a doubt what the Lord wanted us to do.

God gave us the gift of friendship with our housemates, deeper and more precious than anything we can describe. The Lord had us link arms with people and organizations that would further His purposes for years to come. God put our children in an environment where there were people to love and nurture them and provide for them in ways we couldn't. I believe that God even used us to be a blessing and support for others by being where we were.

Living where we did, the load on both William and me was much lighter, and we were both able to concentrate on God's agenda instead of working so hard at living. We were given companionship, support, love, laughter, safety, and provision.

I remember as we traveled to Afghanistan telling the Lord that He was going to need to take care of some big things for us because we only had a short time in this country, and we didn't want to waste all our time learning to live instead of living for Him. God was faithful; and because of our living arrangements, William was able to go to work one week after we arrived. The kids started school just two days after getting there, and within two weeks we were settled and "living" in our "new normal." God knew all along what was needed; He had the big picture in focus.

Philippians 4:11-13

I have learned in whatever state I am, to be content:
I know how to be abased, and I know how to abound.
Everywhere and in all things I have learned both to be
full and to be hungry, both to abound and to suffer need. I
can do all things through Christ who strengthens me.

Letter 14 - Hidden Lessons

As most of you are sleeping, I am sitting at my desk dreaming about a fountain Diet Coke with crushed ice and a hot shower, not necessarily together, just both in the same day. Yesterday, as I was washing my hair, I looked over at the wall outlet where our hot water heater is plugged in and saw smoke coming out of it. When I looked closer, I saw that the outlet was melting and literally running down the wall. Not something you see every day at home, and if you did, your house would be on fire. Fortunately, here all the houses are made of concrete so there is nothing to burn. So, no hot showers for us until the wall is rewired; and here that could take weeks. Back to boiled water and bucket baths. Living in a developing country, we have a saying: "Here, nothing is ever easy or convenient." That pretty much sums it up.

Our bathroom is one big room with a showerhead, a sink, and a toilet all out in the open. Everything is covered in tile, so when I clean things, I just hose down the room and squeegee everything into the drain in the middle of the floor. This week, the plumbing in the house is being redone to replace metal pipes with plastic, and, hopefully, to keep things from freezing this winter. So as I write this, not only do we not have hot water; but I have a hole in the floor that looks all the way down to the first floor bathroom. If I did want to take a shower, I would have to cover the hole with a towel so that the rest of the house would not get a "peep show." All of this construction comes when the house is almost to capacity, too; within three days there will be twenty extra people living in this house and we will be sharing our tiny bathroom with eight people. Not an easy task with all the extra challenges right now.

When I write these letters, I feel like such a complainer; like I am only ever writing about what is hard and challenging. I'm sorry for that because there really are some wonderful things here, too.

Last week in our orientation, we were taught about hospitality in this country. The nationals here are some of the most gracious hosts I will ever meet. There is a great deal of detail and sacrifice that goes into making people feel welcome and honored. When one is invited to a national's home, he is greeted at the door like royalty. He takes his shoes off and is offered slippers to wear while inside. He will be invited to enter their gathering room. Inside the room, there are toshacks (long pillows to sit on) lined around the outside walls of the room. He will be offered the seat farthest from the door, which is a place of honor. For the next several hours, he will be served tea and snacks and eventually a full meal. There are always many different dishes of food (the more dishes there are, the more honored the guest). There is always more food than needed. One should never finish everything on his plate, as the host will feel he is still hungry and fill it again. No one ever leaves a host's home while he is still hungry. Food is a very important part of this culture; it speaks love and honor in a way nothing else does. If one breaks bread with a national, he is considered a dear friend and will always be honored in their family and home. What he probably will not know is that, in many cases, someone in the home will go without food so that the guest may be honored. In this culture, hospitality is truly a sacrificial thing, something of great honor, and should be respected.

Wouldn't it be wonderful if our culture were able to grasp this concept even a little bit? Anyone who takes the time and energy to come to my home should never go away hungry or not knowing how much she is appreciated. Even sharing a simple cup of tea together here binds a friendship. It is said that when a person shares three cups of tea with someone from this country, then she is truly a friend, an honored member of their family; drinking tea together is a sign of relationship.

There is another neat custom here. When we see people we know each day, no matter how many times in a day, we always stop and say hello and then ask them how they are, even if we see them twenty times a day. It would be considered very rude and dishonoring if we were to pass those people again and again and not acknowledge them. There is also a three-kiss greeting when we see a friend, always men to men and women to women; but we should stop, look them in the eye, and kiss first the left cheek, then the right, then back to the left. In our hurried Western mindset, it would be quite difficult to stop so many times a day just to honor someone, but here it represents the fact that relationship is by far the most important element of life. Think if we took the time to honor and respect those closest to us on a much more regular basis how much richer our lives would be. In our Western mindset, tasks are often more important than relationships. It has to do with the way we measure productivity. If we are able to scratch off everything on our lists in a day, then we feel we have truly accomplished something. Here we have to learn to measure productivity differently. Instead of how much we do in a day, maybe it's more about how many people we spoke to in a day or how much time we took to really listen to someone. It's hard for me to grasp sometimes that, in the long run, it's more important what I am than what I do. It's easy to let life suck the important things away from us, letting stuff and schedules get in the way of relationship and people. I think because Westerners tend to live so spread out and isolated from family it's hard for us to let strangers into our lives; it takes a lot of work to build a friendship, to foster relationship. Instead, we default to what makes us feel better about ourselves… tasks, accomplishments. Sometimes building relationship is risky; we have to be vulnerable and transparent. As Westerners, we often feel uncomfortable wondering how people perceive us. In order to really *build a meaningful relationship, we have to trust one another. We have to trust, even through our faults and weaknesses, knowing that there will be times when expectations are not met and hearts will be wounded. But if we persevere, the payoff is huge, the treasure great, and the effort well worth it. I am learning a great lesson from my host country…. relationship and hospitality first, even with my enemies. When done right, my enemies could someday be my friends. An Afghan proverb says:* **The first day you meet, you are friends. The next day you meet, you are brothers.**

Personal Reflection

In God's world, people are always more important than tasks. Think about how many times Jesus stopped and talked with people, healed them, loved them. I'm sure He was often frustrated and felt pulled on. As a human, He probably had plans and agendas but always put them aside for the people around him. People never left Jesus' company feeling anything but loved and accepted. In my heart of hearts, I know that if I will purpose to be obedient to love people, then God will see to it that the right tasks get accomplished. We have to use wisdom and make sure we are putting our time and effort where the Lord would have us. Even though we need to be able to set healthy boundaries, we still have to learn to spend more time investing in eternal things…people!

The Afghan culture taught me to shift my focus in some of these areas. It's not comfortable for me. I am much more at ease with "doing" than "being" and would rather scratch tasks off my list than make myself available to others; but God is helping me in this process. He is helping me see every day where my energy and time will best be invested: in the eternal.

Proverbs 18:24
A man who has friends must himself be friendly, but there is a friend who sticks closer than a brother.

Letter 15 - It's a Small World After All

As I sat down to write, I noticed I could hear the "ice cream man's cart" coming down our street. He's not really a man; he's a young boy riding a bike that has a cooler-type case attached to the front holding local ice cream that he sells to the kids on the street. I have seen the "ice cream man" all over town many times and heard the annoying songs that the carts play. Today, however, I realized that the song that was playing sounded familiar. As I listened for a minute, I had to just laugh as I realized that the song was "It's a Small World After All." What a crazy clash of culture! I'm pretty sure that most locals have never been to Disneyland and have never even heard of the boat ride attraction at the theme park, so where in the world did they get this song? To the locals it means ice cream; to us Westerners it represents a childhood memory of a fantasy land far from anyone's imagination in this country. Wow, it was a crazy moment for me! It really is a small world after all, isn't it?

In two days, we will have been in our host country for a month. It is crazy to realize that time is such a weird thing. How can it go so fast and at the same time drag on and on?

I'm slowly getting to the point that I feel comfortable in my "new normal." Things are feeling more and more routine all the time. There are still times though, as I take my laundry off the line on the roof of our house with a view of the mountains behind me and the city before me, or when I pour the coffee grounds down the toilet because I don't have a garbage disposal, or when I have to prime the hot water before taking a shower, that I remember that life is still pretty abnormal. Maybe I will always feel like this to some extent and maybe that's a good thing. With the realization, at times, that life is challenging and different, it reminds me to be thankful and to keep my heart soft. We, as Westerners, know such an easy life most of the time that I think it can harden us and inhibit us from keeping a soft and compassionate heart toward the "world." I never want to be so consumed with "me" that I can't see the lives of others.

Khalil is an amazing young man who works for the family we live with. He always has a smile on his face, is always dressed in his very best and goes above and beyond to be as kind and generous as he can be. When we are with Khalil, he is always looking out for us, breaking cultural rules by considering that we, as women, are people, too. As I spend time with him though, I realize that his life is anything but easy and comfortable. He is an educated man who used to work for a well known organization, managing and directing people under him and making a lot more money than he does now. Because now there is very little work in this country, Khalil is working as a driver. His English is very good, but he is always working to better it by asking questions and copying what we say. Last week he shared with us that when the Taliban came into the city, he was working at a private compound when it was raided. He tried to protect one of the expats he was with, but he ended up in prison where he was beaten so badly he couldn't walk for months! Khalil is determined to walk in forgiveness and wants people to be drawn to him for his kindness. He lives about fifty kilometers from us; he leaves his home at 5:00 a.m. and takes four taxis in order to get to work by 7:30 a.m. He repeats the process in the afternoon. Khalil is a constant reminder to me that I have nothing to complain about. I look at him and his smile and instantly remember all I have to be grateful for. I also am reminded to walk in grace with people, offering forgiveness even when I feel it's not deserved. I am inspired and challenged by the life that Khalil lives. He is certainly a "rose" in the dust of this land! He is a treasure that I did not expect when I arrived in Afghanistan. Though our lives, language, culture, and faith are vastly different, he is teaching me something each and every day. And when the blinding differences are taken away, we are both simply two of God's creations trying to do the best we can with the life we have been given.

Personal Reflection

There were many Afghans who taught me things about life. God used them over and over again to remind me of important truths. Did you know God uses unlikely people to accomplish His plans? It's weird to think about. We feel that we, as believers, are somehow better than the sinner next to us. Are we better; or do we just live in more revelation? We are sinners too, just sanctified sinners. We are all God's creations and He loves us the same. Why do you think sinners prosper and have blessings in their lives? Because God loves them. The Bible tells us,

> *"Every good gift and every perfect gift is from above; it comes down from the Father of all light, in whom there can be no variation or shadow cast by His turning."* James 1:17 (Amplified)

If ALL good and perfect things are from God, then the good things in sinners' lives must be from Him as well. God will never stop showing Himself faithful to all people.

Don't limit the way the Lord wants to teach and bless you. Don't disregard the goodness of God just because it comes from an unlikely source. God is at work in all of His creations. He loves everyone and wants everyone to be reconciled to Him.

In Afghanistan, those men motivated by an internal code of kindness and morality, who endeavor to live outside themselves attempting to be gracious and merciful, are called "soft-hearted men." Our driver, Mohammed, is one of those men. Mohammed has been connected with our organization for several years, driving for our U.S. doctors and foreign visitors who work with our hospital. He was originally hired because he could speak English and was considered very trustworthy. I met Mohammed for the first time when I visited Kabul five years earlier. There was an instant bond between Mohammed and my husband and even today we feel like family. Because Mohammed speaks English and has had the opportunity to work with foreigners, he displayed great patience and understanding with our "backward" ways.

Mohammed drove my husband to and from work every day. Because of the crazy traffic situation along with the frequent security issues, some days they would spend several hours together talking about life and family. Each Saturday, Mohammed, my husband, and I would spend the day doing our weekly grocery shopping. Some Saturdays we would spend four to five hours together navigating the local shops and bazaars. On these shopping days, Mohammed would graciously entertain my constant bombardment of questions about his culture and religion; and, though it was not acceptable, he had no problem walking side by side with me having open conversations while we shopped for our items. Behind the closed doors of his car, I always felt a sense of warmth and safety while we traveled the uncertain terrain of the city. With Mohammed, I never felt inferior because I was a woman; different, yes, but not inferior. Sometimes it was easy for me to forget Mohammed was an Afghan and even though his speech was heavy with an accent, his thoughts and conversations were often "Western."

When I think about the safety and equality I felt with Mohammed, it's really a bit mind-boggling. Mohammed is not an educated man, at least not in the way we think about education. He never finished school, dropping out in grade eight to work and make money for his family. And though Mohammed can speak several languages fluently, he never learned to read or write in his own language.

Mohammed is not Pashtun and not a stranger to persecution. During the rule of the Taliban, he was a bus driver. Like most developing countries, public transportation is vital to the success of business and retail, as most people cannot afford to own a car. Being a bus driver is a very respectable profession. During the rule of the Taliban, Mohammed was beaten several times for not being aware of the ever-changing rules. In Afghanistan, it is never appropriate for a woman to ride in the front seat of a car with a male driver nor is it ever appropriate for her to ride sitting next to a man on a bus. For that reason, there are "women only" buses and there are buses where the men and women are separated.

On one occasion, Mohammed was stopped, violently pulled from his bus and beaten on the side of the road because he did not realize the Taliban had made a rule that all women must be in the back of the bus, not the front. A week later he was again dragged off the bus and beaten because the Taliban officer informed him that now the women must all be at the front of the bus. In reality, there had been no rule change; it was just an excuse to take a man off the bus and beat him. During this same time, Mohammed's home was raided several times, and all of his possessions and those of this family members were pillaged and things stolen. It became apparent that for the family's safety, they must relocate to Pakistan. So, during the second year of the Taliban's rule, Mohammed snuck his parents, brothers with their wives and children, and himself across the border into Pakistan. Also, while in Pakistan the men in the family worked at large carpet factories, hand-weaving the beautiful carpets that adorn all Afghan homes. While in Pakistan, Mohammed and his brothers all learned English, a skill that would later provide them with very good income.

Shortly after Mohammed and his family returned to Afghanistan, he was introduced to our organization and began driving for us. As I stated earlier, Mohammed is a "soft-hearted man." He lives by an internal moral code that few Afghans recognize. Though his life has been riddled with abuse and fear, Mohammed has chosen to believe the best in people and endeavors to live a life of integrity and charity. During the long hours of conversations William and I shared with Mohammed, not only would I ask him endless questions about his culture and country, but he would do the same with us. He was always very intrigued with the relationship between my husband and me. A "love" marriage is almost unheard of in this part of the world. Since almost all marriages are arranged, it is common for the wedding day to be the first time a bride and groom meet. Marriage is a business contract and is used to produce male children in hopes of bringing honor and power to the family. Mohammed spent many hours asking us questions and observing my husband and me "partner" in our relationship. He was intrigued by the fact that my husband was interested in my opinion and respected my ideas and input. In the Afghan culture, the wife's job is to cook, clean, and produce children. The man's job is to work, bring home supplies for his wife and children and their home, and foster his own social agenda. The man does all the shopping. It's common to see men in the market buying women's undergarments since some of the wives are often forbidden to leave their homes. For Mohammed, spending so much time with a man who loves and honors his wife, it was challenging and intriguing. Just a short time before we left Afghanistan, Mohammed shared something surprising to us. He told us he had decided his wife would be allowed to wear only the chadar (loose-fitting head scarf) that the foreign women wear; he would no longer require her to wear a burka, the cloak which is worn in public that covers the face and body. Mohammed made the decision to allow his wife to choose whether or not she wanted to veil. In Afghan culture, this was a revolutionary decision, because women are never given choices and certainly not respected enough to consider what they may want. After being with us, Mohammed had made it a priority to learn to think differently about certain things. He also told us he was using a good portion of his salary to pay for his daughter to attend a private school. This was another revolutionary choice since, as previously mentioned, most young girls are not allowed to attend school, especially if it means taking a spot at a private school normally reserved for a boy. Attending a private school would mean Mohammed's daughter would receive a far better education than in the government schools because she would learn to read and write, not only in Dari but also in English.

One night, while eating dinner with Mohammed's family, he had his oldest daughter join us to demonstrate her reading and writing skills in English along with working some math problems for us. Even though Mohammed lacks the skills his daughter possesses, he is one of the smartest Afghans I know. He was so proud of his daughter's skills that night and couldn't help grinning from ear to ear as we all clapped for what she had accomplished. The fact that Mohammed's daughter was gaining skills he himself did not possess wasn't viewed by him as dishonoring. Instead, it filled Mohammed with pride, and he saw in his daughter hope for his family and his country. He also didn't care that his life would be in danger if the Taliban ever returned or if it was discovered he was not following cultural norms. His courageous decisions might even mean that both he and his daughter could become targets to be killed. For his nation to change, Mohammed understands that the children of today, and not exclusively the boys, need knowledge and opportunity. My heart wanted to burst with happiness as I watched Mohammed with his daughter that special night.

One day Mohammed said to us, "You are better Muslims than we are. We lie and steal and cheat one another and still do prayers and give to the poor, but you live what you believe." It was a sobering and exciting moment for us as we realized Mohammed was starting to consider that there might be other ways of looking at things. For a Muslim, not only is Islam their religion, it is their culture. A Muslim is a Muslim because he was born a Muslim; there is no free will or choice in the matter. All Muslims are brought up believing there is only one way to look at life. A person cannot think and decide for himself; everything has already been decided because of Allah. If someone dies, it is Allah's will. If someone lives, it is Allah's will. If someone has money, it is Allah's will. If someone is poor, it is Allah's will.

As I sit writing today, I am distracted by thinking of all the beautiful people of Afghanistan who die every day without the truth. I just finished reading an email telling us about the death of another Afghan friend; we have lost several. Each one is a representation of the lost men and women of this land. The horrible suffering they have endured during life will pale by comparison with the horrific suffering they will experience for eternity. As I stared at the beautiful face of our friend in a picture we took with him just days before leaving Afghanistan, I couldn't help but reflect on the many conversations we shared over the past year. I think of the dinners and meetings spent talking about insignificant things: small talk about life, politics, and family. However, we never talked of the truth that would have given him true liberty.

Talking about faith in a closed country is a difficult and complicated thing. Yes, we talked about principles and morals and concepts surrounding our truth; but we never felt we could say, "Without Jesus, this is all in vain." The risk to us and to others is great. I heard it said among the foreign community, "Be led before you open your mouth; someone else's life is a precious thing to risk." But isn't that exactly what we did? We were hesitant to risk our own comfort and safety for someone else to know the truth. We took a gamble that there would be another time or place, a safer, more convenient, opportunity. Our friend is the one who will suffer now. What do we really have to lose? Our earthly lives? That is a small price to pay for another's eternity. Our eternity through the work of Jesus Christ on the cross is only gain. Our precious friend lost everything and will never have another opportunity. Our only comfort is knowing that God is not willing that any man perish (2 Peter 2:3) and that He has made Himself known to all men through His creation (Romans 1:20).

There is a layer of fear, deception, and oppression that hangs over Afghanistan like a thick cloud. The heaviness makes it difficult to think straight. The fear is tangible. The darkness is so heavy that it can be completely paralyzing, like an animal caught in the crosshairs of a gun, unable to move. Those of us with what we consider light who lived among those living in darkness would often pray for our light to brighten the path enough for those walking in darkness to take a step toward seeing things differently. As I reflect on my friend's death, I can't help but wonder if I could have been more deliberate in revealing the light and truth. Really, I have nothing to lose, and my unbelieving friends have everything to gain. I know others would argue that things in closed countries are really not that simple; but as I ponder today's tragic event, I can't help but think they might be!

As I struggle with what is and what could have been during our time in Afghanistan, where freedom and liberty, especially in my faith, are extremely limited, I am forced to consider what I will do when those limitations no longer exist. What do I do when I have the freedom to say and do as I please? In Afghanistan, questioning one's Muslim faith runs the risk of imprisonment and even death. But here in America, what do we need to fear? That someone will think we are pushy, or crazy, or obnoxious? It's such a small price to pay for someone's eternity. Why is it so hard for us to consider telling strangers that Jesus loves them? Why can we so easily go about our lives ignoring the lost people dying every day around us?

A Moment Lost

Years ago, when our family was living in Ghana, West Africa, I traveled home for the birth of my sister's first baby. I was sitting in the airport in London reading a book when a Muslim woman about my age came and sat across from me with her young son. At this time in my life, I didn't know much about the Muslim faith and what I did know made me a bit uneasy. As I sat across from this woman, I felt the Spirit nudge me to give her a small New Testament I was carrying with me and simply say, "God wants you to know that He loves you." I wrestled with God about giving the woman the

Bible. I argued with Him that this wasn't a good idea because she probably wasn't allowed to read it, and I could cause her harm by giving it to her; and she could be very offended. The intense conversation went on and on. I know it was just a matter of minutes, but it felt like hour. My palms were hot and sticky, and my heart was racing like crazy. By the time I had almost talked myself into giving the woman the Bible, I looked up, and she was gone. I had missed my chance. In the years following that incident, I was introduced to Afghanistan and began to study Islam. I learned how to establish relationships with Muslims and also learned that reading a New Testament is not illegal or wrong for a Muslim; in fact, it is encouraged, though few know that.

In Islam, the New Testament is called the Injeel and is seen as the teaching of a sinless prophet, Issa (Jesus). Jesus is recognized as a very powerful prophet and is even believed to be a sinless man, born of a virgin, who ascended to heaven and who will one day return to earth. The biggest difference between what Christians and Muslims believe is whether or not Jesus was the Son of God, and therefore, whether or not He is God. Muslims are encouraged in the Koran to read the Injeel to know more about this prophet. However, the "culture" of Islam states that only men are permitted to read the Koran and only if it is read in its original text, Arabic. Most men here cannot speak Arabic and must rely on the mullahs (teachers) to translate what the Koran says. The Injeel, however, is not part of the Koran; it is what is referred to as supplemental teaching, good works of writing, but not inspired by God. Most men are never taught that they can read the Injeel themselves, and they certainly would not pass that information on to their wives.

As I reflect on this incident, I know now that it would not have been inappropriate at all to have given her that New Testament. And if I had said, "God wants you to know He loves you," it probably would have been very meaningful to her because Muslims refer to God as Allah. If I am being completely honest, it wasn't necessary for me to have all the additional information I have since obtained to make the right choice at that particular moment. God was asking me to simply obey Him. I did not obey and the woman left without the New Testament in her hand. I asked God to forgive me for my disobedience and prayed He would send another laborer across that woman's path. I was so distracted by what could have happened or how she might respond to me that I missed the opportunity altogether.

God is mighty and powerful, and He can do anything to present truth to people; however, in most situations, He chooses to use us. We are the hands and feet of Jesus. He left us with the Holy Spirit to empower us to do His good works. We need to trust Him and not allow our fear to stop us from doing what He wants done for His beautiful, precious people. I often reflect on that day in the London airport and wonder how things might have been different if I had been obedient. Would that woman have read for herself about the truth of Jesus, surrendered her life to Him, and been responsible for the salvation of her family? We need to listen to the Holy Spirit and trust Him enough to be bold in walking out what He has for us. The world is counting on us. Our neighbor, the woman in line at the grocery store, our co-worker, the homeless man at the intersection we drive by each day—their eternity may depend on us!

Proverbs 11:30
The fruit of the righteous is a tree of life,
and he who wins souls is wise.

Letter 16 - Happy Anniversary to Us!

Happy Anniversary to us! One month today in our host country. Wow, a lot has changed for us indeed. I'm still coming to grips with it all and maybe I never will completely, but I think that's how it is supposed to be. Life is a journey, filled with change and adaptation. If we get too routine and predictable, we should worry. How can we change, grow, and mature unless we stretch and step out some? I, for one, am very grateful for the opportunity to be more than I thought I could be. I'm grateful for the chance for my faith to grow, to love deeper, and to live wider than I thought possible.

There is an international team here right now, a group of doctors. Their team coming has brought a breath of fresh air and encouraged us to push harder. This week, the team was teaching a workshop at the hospital, challenging everyone to be the best they can be in medicine and in character, both a hard feat in this country. Yesterday I went with the team to the hospital and was invited to have tea with the female physicians in their private "all girl" room. As we entered the room, all the women took off their chadars (scarves). One girl who veils completely took off her veil and for the first time I could see how beautiful she was. For the short time we were together, we were just all women - moms and wives sharing stories of how hard it is to work outside the home and balance life. I was an instant celebrity when they found out that I have six children and three of them sons. It was beautiful, when the scarves and veils were dropped and the door closed, to see how similar we were. Though there are cultural things that separate us, the bottom line was that we were all women trying to be the best we could be as we balanced the struggles of life. We laughed and told stories; it was a precious time for me. I look forward to more times like that. I promised the ladies I would come more often and have tea.

I think it's important to point out that these women are amazing examples of courage and tenacity in this county. These women have been through medical school, a feat almost impossible for a female who is married and has children. On top of working long hours at the hospital, they go home and cook and clean and serve their husbands and children. One of the women travels an hour in each direction to get to work and must bring her baby and a hired helper to the hospital with her, as she has no help in the home. She uses all of her salary for travel and childcare. Each of these women carries a big load at the hospital, assisting with deliveries and women's medical issues because the male doctors cannot treat female issues in this society. As I look at these bright, beautiful women, I am amazed at the commitment and courage they all have to face: the hardships of this culture and the pursuit of knowledge in order to help their country. I was challenged and humbled to be in their company.

The doctors, both men and women, desire to better their English. Though all do quite well, they want to be excellent in English; so they asked me to be their teacher. I think I may take them up on the offer. We have worked it out so that maybe twice a week or so, I will go to the hospital and hold English classes; and then our driver will pick me up; then we will pick up the children from school. It's a crazy revelation that I may have something to give these very bright, educated physicians. I look forward to the teaching times and the exchange of ideas and values.

So today is not only important because it is the anniversary of our arrival, it's also important because it marks the end of the first quarter of school. Today we had parent-teacher conferences with all of Laney's and Hank's teachers at their new school. We were thrilled to find out that they are doing very well and, though the school is quite academically challenging, both are holding their own. Hank has actually been moved up a grade level in both math and science. I can't tell you how relieved I am that they have adjusted so well and are excelling, even in the shadow of such a huge transition.

I mentioned that we have guests right now and how fun it is to have a taste of home brought by familiar faces. Our daughter sent several items to us with the team to make life a bit easier. Included in the care package that came were dish cloths and cocoa and popcorn, but the treasured item was a shower curtain. It's super cute with blue and green polka dots and makes the bathroom look very Western and cheerful, as well as helping to contain some of the water that freely flows over the entire bathroom floor. It's absolutely amazing how such a small thing like a shower curtain can completely transform how things work and feel around here; it's so the little things!

Personal Reflection

God is the master of "little things." He knows us better than we know ourselves and, if we will allow Him to, He will continually surprise us with little treasures that feed our hearts. God understands that we live in a fallen world and that we are incomplete and fallen without Him. He knows that life can be hard and challenging and He wants us to know that He cares about us and the little things in our lives that we care about.

Years ago, when our children were little, we bought two chocolate Labrador retriever puppies for them. A week after getting the pups, we realized that one of them was not responding to her name or coming when we called her. We took the puppy to the veterinarian and discovered that the puppy's eardrums were malformed and she was completely deaf. The vet encouraged us to have the puppy put down, saying that it could be dangerous having her around small children. My husband and I talked about it and thought that it was not honoring to the Lord to have something killed just because it wasn't perfect; the dog was not suffering and could live a relatively normal life. We felt putting the dog down would not be a good example to the children. When we told the children about the puppy, our second daughter Joy said she wanted to pray and ask God to heal her puppy. For three days, Joy walked around with that little puppy, praying over her, saying, "Thank you Jesus, that Sadie can hear; thank you Lord, for healing Sadie." On the third day, we were sitting in the kitchen having breakfast, the phone rang and I noticed that Sadie turned her head toward the sound. We all got excited and started calling Sadie, watching her run to us over and over. The next day we took Sadie to the vet, and the vet looked at me with a puzzled expression on his face and said, "I can't explain it; Sadie's ear drums are still completely malformed, but she is hearing perfectly!" Praise the Lord! He had healed Sadie! God cares about what we care about. The story of Sadie was told many times during the fourteen years she was with us. The story astonished many and perplexed others, but it was an example of how much God loves us and how much He cares about what we care about.

Don't miss the little gifts that God puts in your life just to bless you. He wants to let you know that He cares about you, and He cares about what you care about. It may be something dramatic like Sadie's healing or just a polka dot shower curtain; but no matter how big or small, God wants you to know His love for you!

While in Afghanistan, one of the greatest privileges I was given was having an opportunity to build relationships with the women where my husband worked. I know this seems almost impossible in light of what I just described. Each one of these women is gifted with intelligence and, because their fathers allowed them to attend school, their gifts were noticed. When they were given a standardized test, each woman was allowed into the career of medicine because of her high scores. In spite of cultural and societal pressure, they have pressed forward, determined to become educated and trained to make a difference in the lives of their people.

The Afghan culture forbids male doctors from treating and caring for women, especially in the birth process. Because of this, the maternal and fetal morbidity rates here are some of the highest in the world. Women and children die every day simply because they do not have qualified health care providers to care for them. The women physicians are often required to do the obstetrical work for the hospital and be available for the female patients who come to the clinic. In addition to being doctors, these women are wives and mothers, so they are required to cook, clean, and take care of their families while working anywhere from eight to twenty-four hour shifts each day. The demands on these women are great. Their resolve, courage, and commitment was a challenge to me. I believe they will play a very key role in helping their country transition out of the current chaos.

Matthew 6:31-33

Therefore do not worry, saying, 'What shall we eat?' or 'What shall we drink?' or 'What shall we wear?' For after all these things the Gentiles seek. For your heavenly Father knows that you need all these things. But seek first the kingdom of God and His righteousness, and all these things shall be added to you.

CHAPTER 6 – Life Through the Broken Glass

I Corinthians 13:12-13

For now we see in a mirror, dimly, but then face to face. Now I know in part, but then I shall know just as I also am known. And now abide faith, hope, love, these three; but the greatest of these is love.

Letter 17 - I Am So Sick of Dirt

I am so sick of dirt! Not a great way to start, I know; but it's the truth. I'm just so sick of wiping dust off EVERYTHING!! Three days ago the "winter winds" hit. There is a Dari name for them, but I can't remember what it is. Basically, all the dust from the rest of the world blows across this country and behind the dust comes the colder air of winter. We have had three dust storms in the last 24 hours and the temperature has dropped 20 degrees from last week. Now when I say a dust storm, I mean literally a storm like a thunderstorm, only with dirt. When it's going on, I cannot see across the street and with every window and door shut tight there is still enough dirt that gets in that I can taste it and feel it in my hair like someone has dumped baby powder on me. We can feel the grit in our teeth and when we wash our hands or take a shower, the water is black with the dirt that washes off. I can't tell you how sad it makes me when I wipe down every hard surface and wipe off every single thing sitting out just to wake up the next morning and have it covered with enough dust to be able to write my name in the dirt again. Here's a fun fact for you. Did you know that Afghanistan has the highest percentage of aerosolized feces in the air of any country in the world? Great! Not only do I have fat bottom sheep walking up and down my road, their poop is now all over my furniture and countertops and even our toothbrushes! GREAT! Let's just hope it adds to the protein in our diet, because we can certainly use it. The carb load we get every day just isn't hacking it... but that's another letter.

Our team left on Friday, and I have to admit I had a little breakdown; okay, it wasn't really so little, but anyway... I couldn't believe how sad I was; I mean - I am. I think with them here I felt like there was a piece of home living with me. When they left, I suddenly felt so sad for everyone and everything in my life back home; I started to realize how much I really miss:

- *My kids*
- *My family and friends*

- *My church*
- *Diet Coke with crushed ice*
- *Hot baths*
- *Caldrea kitchen counter cleaner*
- *Pumpkin spice coffee creamer*
- *My bed*
- *Long handled brooms and real mops*
- *Putting used toilet paper in the TOILET*
- *My hairdresser*
- *Bella Vita*
- *Picking up the phone and touching base with everyone I love whenever I want*
- *Date nights at the movies*
- *Frozen Yogurt*
- *Long walks in the park*
- *Driving*
- *Running errands*
- *My dishwasher*
- *My washing machine and dryer*
- *My vacuum*
- *Real Windex*
- *Meat*
- *Reese's peanut butter cups*
- *Ketchup*
- *Sandwiches with turkey and cheese*
- *Working outside in my flower beds*
- *Duke and Daisy (my Great Danes)*
- *My fireplace*
- *Fall decorations*
- *Football*
- *TV*
- *Central heat*

Okay, really that's pretty pathetic. I need to stop!

I am healthy, blessed, and provided for. I'm just feeling a bit sorry for myself, which is ridiculous. Look what I have:

- *A house to live in*
- *Running water, both hot and cold*
- *A Western toilet that is indoors*
- *A kitchen inside my house*
- *A stove*
- *A refrigerator*
- *All the supplies I need to feed my family*
- *A hot shower every day (well, most days)*
- *A warm bed to sleep in*
- *Extra blankets if I need them*
- *A bedroom separate from my children*
- *Warm clothes to wear*
- *More than one pair of shoes*
- *A coat, gloves and boots for the snow*
- *My husband home by 5:00 p.m. every day with a three-day weekend*
- *A beautiful view of the mountains*
- *Friends from all over the world*
- *As much rice and naan bread as I can eat*
- *A yard with grass*
- *Roses growing nine feet tall*
- *A view of the very funny fat bottom sheep that live next door*
- *Pomegranates that cost twenty cents instead of $3 apiece*
- *Figs on a string*
- *Windows with glass that separate us from more things than I can list*
- *Enough money to pay our bills and take care of our family*
- *A husband who is kind and considerate and does not beat me*
- *A father-in-law who does not make me wear a burka*
- *A school for my children to attend and actually learn the skills they need to go to college*

- *Full-time security*
- *A wardrobe of beautiful chadars that I can match with every-thing I wear*
- *The sweetest grapes and bananas that you have ever eaten within a half a block from our house*
- *Time to myself when I can read and write and actually reflect on the blessings in my life*

How blessed I am! I do miss some things from home and wish I could access them a bit more frequently, but I am a blessed and happy woman who wouldn't trade this amazing journey for anything!

Personal Reflection

It's all about perspective! When I take time to list the things I have, I find I don't miss the things I don't have nearly as much!

A friend who is a pastor in America preached a sermon on keeping your "bread basket" in front of you. He talked about how the blessings in our life are like bread in a basket, nourishment and comfort for our lives. There is nothing like hot homemade bread spread with sweet creamy butter and jam. The smell, the texture, and the taste are all so satisfying; that is how the blessings of God are in our lives. They are not always what we recognize right in front of us; but if I take some time to think about them and list them, I am always surprised at how many there are and how rich my life is because of them. Next time you find yourself sad and lonely for certain things that are "missing" in your life, take a moment to get a piece of paper out and write down all the things you do have. I'll bet you will be much more surprised at what you have been blessed with than you are sad for what you don't have. If you take some time, you will feel warm and satisfied and comforted; and you will thank the Lord for His goodness.

1 Timothy 6:6-8

Now godliness with contentment is great gain. For we brought nothing into this world, and it is certain we can carry nothing out. And having food and clothing, with these we shall be content.

Letter 18 - Update on the Family

I realize that I haven't really let everyone know what the rest of the family has been up to lately. So here is an update.

My husband has been doing really well. The hospital work is going great, though always slow in a third world country, but it is most certainly moving forward. He heads out to the hospital around 7:00 each morning; he makes a half-hour drive to the hospital building. He then does rounds with the doctors and catches up on what has gone on during the night. After lunch, there is patient care and teaching and clinical updating, sometimes taught by him and sometimes by guests. When not teaching, he is in meetings. Right now, they are working on a couple of special projects. One is trying to put together a clinic for a community near the river that needs local medical care. Another project is trying to set up an organized clinic site for the expatriate community along with protocols for those needing medical attention outside of a clinic setting or after hours. He has taken care of two appendicitis situations for expats just this week, as well as some other patients: many of the expat families' children and family members are suffering with flu and colds and upper respiratory infections (quite common with all the dust). There is a need for good medical care for the NGO (non-governmental organization) workers here as well as the nationals. Though we all live just a 15-minute drive from an international military compound where there is a state-of-the-art medical facility, we can't use it unless we are missing a limb or have a personal military connection—which is a bit of a disappointment. There are so many foreigners in the country that need medical care at times, with only a wall separating us from all things Western. Hence, the need for a community health center for expats.

One of my husband's personal gifts is diplomacy, so a big part of what he is involved in right now is bridging gaps and combining efforts to make the medical community and NGO community work more efficiently. We have had the opportunity to meet with some very influential people in this country, a great gift when trying to get things done. "Favor" is all around William right now, so he is excited each and every day to see what his encounters will hold.

The kids are doing amazingly. Not once in our five weeks here have I heard one word of "I miss this or that" or "I want to go home." Honestly, I think they are doing better than we adults sometimes. School is going really well for both of them. The academics are quite challenging and keeping them on their toes. Hank has been moved up to an 8th grade math class. (We have Mrs. L to thank for that, helping us hone in on some concepts in algebra as we prepared to leave.)

Hank is playing soccer and basketball after-school and is quite involved in a youth group here for teens. Laney is in ballet and has a singing solo part in the musical "Annie"; she is enjoying her after school music club a lot. Laney has also landed a babysitting job a couple times a week for her ballet teacher; quite the big girl for sure. My whole "little" family is home to our apartment by 5:00 p.m. each day, and we have about a half hour of sunlight to play badminton or soccer in the yard. After dinner, we settle into our little house for homework and reading and sometimes a movie on the wall with the big projector and popcorn.

As for me, I spend most days here in my little "hobbit" house. Each day I wash everything down to control the dust, cleaning the floors and washing dishes. Sometimes I have time to bake and have cookies or brownies ready when the kids get home. I also usually have a chance to catch up on emails and do some writing if the internet is cooperating. I have been invited to several homes for tea and to visit their projects. So far I have been asked to teach at school, help with the musical, teach aerobics, help build curriculum for the physically and mentally challenged here with an NGO project, and to teach English. Though it's wonderful to feel there are places to plug in, the lack of independence and transportation difficulties are certainly a challenge. Like home, it would be really easy to get "busy" doing a lot of good things and never really honing in on the "right" thing; so I am taking my time to learn to live here and evaluate exactly what I should put my hand to during these upcoming months. Right now I am feeling strongest about teaching English. Not only would it work transportation-wise, but I also feel it may have the most impact long term. I feel this may be an open door to developing some relationships and fostering good cultural and experiential exchanges.

I go to a tap dance class once a week that I am enjoying very much. My housemate also goes with me. It's a great opportunity for female fellowship as well as some exercise. Exercise is really hard to come by here, especially for women. I can't even go outside for a walk except to the end of our road and even then I can never go alone. The diet here is very high in carbs with little protein, so if I don't make a plan to move a bit more, I will go back home looking like the fat bottom sheep that live next door!

Every day that we are here brings us closer to a "new normal." Each day it's easier to go through the day without every task taking a conscious effort to accomplish. It is getting cold quite fast though, and we are on another learning curve. Last night was the first night to sleep with red rubber hot water bottles. We find ourselves looking for the warm spots coming through the windows during the day to take the chill off. Within another week or so we will be bringing the buxari (stoves) into the house and hooking them up. With the arrival of the buxaries, there will be yet another learning curve and more chores added to our days: keeping the fires going and the wood hauled up to our third floor penthouse.

So that's a little rundown on our family. Here is a taste of what is happening at home. The other children are all doing very well at home. Joy and Mitchell and Alex are all pushing hard in school, working on academics, projects, sports, and their social lives. Emma loves her new school and new job and is doing an amazing job taking care of all our responsibilities in America. What incredible young men and women they all are!

Personal Reflection

Because living in Afghanistan seems like such a novelty, many of our friends felt that our days must be dramatic and extraordinary. In reality, though our surroundings were dramatic and at times very different than our home life, most days we lived very ordinary lives. I took care of the home and the responsibilities there. The children went to school and my husband went to work. We visited friends on occasion and went to church every Friday. Our free time was spent with the children, reading or playing, and spending time with our housemates. Our days were routine and predictable, slower paced and easier than at home, and we loved every minute of it.

We experienced extraordinary things as well; instead of snow days we had security days when the kids would stay home from school because security in the city was unstable. We had bomb drills instead of tornado drills. We had to go through pat downs and metal detectors to enter grocery stores and restaurants, and our church meetings were actually in a house. There were machine-gun-carrying guards at every public venue and international soldiers driving the streets. There were no fast food restaurants, and everything we ate had to be cooked from scratch. There were no convenience stores or movie theaters, no department stores or craft stores. But life, though a bit slower and more routine, was rich and full.

Psalm 107:41-43
*Yet He sets the poor on high, far from affliction, and makes
their families like a flock. The righteous see it and rejoice, and
all iniquity stops its mouth. Whoever is wise will observe these
things, and they will understand the loving kindness of the Lord.*

Letter 19 - What Does it Mean to be Content?

*Today I have been pondering the meaning of contentment. What
does it truly mean? I think for me it's learning to live each day in its
own moments, enjoying all that the days hold and not looking ahead
to what is to come. I am learning it really doesn't have anything to
do with things, only with my heart and me. I think I am pretty used
to living each day looking ahead to the next event, project, deadline,
vacation, purchase, or encounter. Our days are marked by what we
cross off on a calendar. Each day we live looking forward to the things
to come, not taking much time to just enjoy what is right in front of us.
We spend our free time catching up on the things we don't have time
for during our "work" time, and our "work" time trying to shovel out
of the stuff that fills our future. My new country is teaching me some
new perspectives on contentment. In the West, we are bombarded with
images and ideas about never having enough. We are presented with
needs that we didn't even know we had; the newest, best, and latest of
any and every item I can think of. Can you ever remember going to a
movie or watching something on TV when you weren't assaulted with
items that make your life easier or better or assist you in saving time,
money, or energy? No matter where we look, there is something new
we need to buy. How many of us can actually go into Wal-Mart and
come out with only what we went in for? Need is so relative, isn't it?
What I "need" back home is totally different than what I need here…
or is it? Why aren't my needs the same in both places? I need shelter,
clothing, food, relationships, air, and water. Anything beyond these
things is really a want.*

As I have been setting up house here, it has been so nice to downsize and learn to live with less. I have a much smaller house with fewer things. However, in my quest to make a home, I have realized that I am still carrying my Western mindset with me. I went to an expat yard sale this weekend. Yard sales happen quite frequently here because of the high degree of turnover of families. That old saying of "one man's trash is another man's treasure" springs to life here. As I went to the yard sale, there was not one thing I needed. I left an hour later, however, with a car full of things I wanted. As I was trying to find space in my tiny little house for all the new "necessities," I found myself thinking about this word "contentment." Now each and every one of the items we brought home I could justify as to why we needed them. A kitchen table, for our landing, that is super cute and now has become the "catch-all" for stuff instead of a place to eat. The couch for the kids' room because they need a place to hang out and read, though the couch in our room has been working just fine. The two bottles of Febreze because it's "American," even though the local air freshener has been working fine (though it smells a bit like a perfume you would find at the dollar store). The four new chadars because they were colors we didn't have, even though Laney and I have more than many nationals will own in a lifetime. A big box of oatmeal, even though we already have two, just because we are afraid we might not find them at the bazaar later. You get the idea. Even though I have been very happy in my little "hobbit" house with everything I could possibly need, I still found more things to stick in my space. This woman is still a slave to the "more is better" mentality. I have realized that I really enjoy the "hunt" for things and then gathering things my family might need or want for later. Now don't misread me; there is balance in all of this. I am American not Afghan, and there are certain comforts and wants that just help me stay in this hard country longer. However, do I really need two teapots? I can only use one at a time. Twenty chadars? There are only seven days in a week. That's a different one for almost a whole month, a bit excessive even by my standards.

This journey has made me much more in tune with why and how I do things; each day brings an opportunity to reevaluate my motives and actions. Is it okay to have a dozen of a certain thing just because I can? Maybe it is, if I can have the right heart attitude and if I am willing to not hold on to things too tightly or let them dominate my thinking. I don't know; I'm just wrestling with it all. It is a constant exercise in humility and self-evaluation to ask myself on a daily basis - "What do I need?" "What do I want?" "What should I be sharing with others?" I believe that all that we have that is good and perfect in our lives comes from God Himself and is meant never to just heap upon ourselves but to be shared with others. If I really believe this, then I need to be learning to hold a bit looser to things and see everything that passes through my hands as being temporary. I just want to keep myself in a position to rule my things, not let them rule me.

As I have been pondering this concept of contentment, I have also been realizing that it means something different to each of us. Each individual as well as culture has different meanings for this word. I realized that, as I came to this country, there was an automatic mindset that if the people of this country had all the advantages and gadgets and modern conveniences as I have in my home country, they would all be so much better off and so much happier. I am quickly realizing, though, that my thoughts are all wrong. There are many cultures, this one included, that are quite content without the modern conveniences to which I am accustomed. Now there are a lot of reasons for this, and I don't really have time to go into them; but sometimes people are not open to change simply because it's unnerving and uncomfortable. Other times, they truly believe there is nothing wrong with the way they do things. For example, Miriam, our house help here in Afghanistan, comes to our home each and every day. We are teaching her ways to clean and wash and iron and do things the way we are most accustomed to and often feel is best. No matter how many times we show her how to do things, there are just some things that she won't change. For instance, Miriam insists on ironing on the floor where she can squat. Every time I look at her doing this while the ironing board stands against the wall, I am just amazed at why she prefers it. And no matter how many times we show her how to

121

use a Western mop, she continually goes back to using a rag on her hands and knees. When we would go into our bathroom after Miriam has used it, we would see footprints all over the seat where she insists on standing on the rim of the toilet instead of sitting. Now Miriam doesn't do this because she is uneducated; she does this because she finds sitting on a toilet seat where other people have sat completely unsanitary and gross. We are a just a bit too full of ourselves when we think about how advanced and capable and "content" we are in our first world surroundings. Don't get me wrong; I wouldn't trade my Western toilet or mop or ironing board in for anything. I'm just being challenged to look at life a bit differently now!

As I head into this next week, I want to be more and more aware of how and why I do things and why I believe the things I do. I want to be open to new ways of thinking and always see myself as no better than the person next to me. Who knows, maybe I'll learn a few things along the way.

Personal Reflection

I learned a lot of things along the way, but this lesson of not thinking too highly of myself was probably one of the biggest. We have no idea what lies behind the lives of the people we meet, what they have lived through or what their perspectives are. Our job is not to judge others or even to change them. Rather our job is to pray for them and love them. Our job is to ask the Holy Spirit to reveal truth to us, the real truth, not what we perceive to be truth; His truth, and then to ask what He would have us do with that truth. Jesus said in Matthew 7:1, "Do not judge and criticize and condemn others, so that you may not be judged and criticized and condemned yourselves."

I don't know about you, but for me being criticized and judged by others when they don't know what is going on is one of life's most painful experiences. Here is scripture that clearly states that we shouldn't do that, so it won't be done to us! It's not our job; not our responsibility. God does not need us to be the judge in life. He has sent the Holy Spirit to do that. He can, however, lead us to teach and impart wisdom if we are willing; but we must do so with an attitude of obedience and love, not arrogance and judgment.

Proverbs 16:18
Pride goes before destruction, and a haughty spirit before a fall.

Letter 20 - Our Journey to School

I just got home from taking the children to school; I thought it might be interesting for you to know how we do it. When I take the kids to school, I travel with my driver, Issa. He picks us up at our house and drives us the two kilometers to school. Issa's car always smells so good. After several weeks I asked him, "How come your car always smells so nice? Is it a kind of car freshener?" He smiled and answered, "No, I think it's me; I have nice soap. " Hank always gets to sit in the front, as he is the oldest son. Women and girls must always sit in the back of vehicles. Even when it's just me in the car, I must always ride in the back and, of course, always be covered with a chapan (overcoat) and chadar (scarf). The roads are very busy with traffic in the mornings and our two-lane road sometimes turns into four or five lanes. Also, when we are turning out of our street, we must merge into the traffic from the left side through the oncoming cars. We do not wait at the corner and turn left when it's clear. If we did, we would still be there hours later. Now picture merging onto any busy road from the wrong direction. Yeah, it's crazy every morning and afternoon. I just close my eyes and wait. There is a secret language here when driving, a language spoken only with horns and hand signals. Each driver knows exactly what it all means and knows how close he can get to a car before braking. It's not the Driver's Education rule of a car length for every ten miles per hour you are moving either. The rule here seems to be if we don't hit another car, we're okay. Sometimes as we are going through a round-about, we are so close that I could reach out and touch the person in the car next to me. Now with all this closeness, there is ample opportunity for people to stare at me, which happens all the time. Yesterday, as we were waiting to turn, a man was crossing the street. As he passed our car, he stopped and bent down just a few inches from the window and stood and stared at me for several minutes. When we started moving, he simply moved to the other side of the car and stared some more. Now men don't look at me here like I'm something beautiful to behold; they look at me like I'm a good beef cow or fat bottom sheep. I can't really explain it, but it's more like they are checking out a piece of equipment than appreciating that I am someone of the opposite sex.

After we merge into oncoming traffic, we must still navigate through two more very busy intersections before arriving at school. Both intersections are often congested with twenty-plus cars trying to turn in four different directions. As we inch our way into the whirlpool, we honk our horn and stay steady on the gas. If we stop, we will lose our place and have to start over. It's a talent that, I fear, takes years to master. Fortunately, Issa is a pro and we have always been able to navigate through the "washing machine" of traffic. As we travel the main street, there are hundreds of people waiting for buses or riding their bikes or just walking, trying to get to work or school. There are food vendors and tiny markets selling all kinds of things. One day I saw a man pushing a cart filled with wheelbarrows stacked upside down five rows high. Another day I watched a butcher cut off the hooves and head of a cow right on the sidewalk. One of our favorite sights in the morning is the young school girls walking to the government school. There are literally hundreds of young girls, ages 5-15, all dressed in black chapans and white chadars, walking hand in hand. It's actually quite breathtaking, considering only a few short years ago girls were not allowed to go to school.

After the two intersections, we travel down a dirt road usually lined with donkeys and carts full of fruits and vegetables ready for the day's markets. The road is full of potholes and is very, very dusty. On one side of the road is a beautiful house with a ten-foot wall around it. A politician of this country lives there and in front is one of the only patches of green grass I have seen in the city. There are four armed military guards that are always out front, and on sunny days I can see them sitting around a table drinking tea while holding their machine guns. The table even has a red and white checked tablecloth on it!

On the left side of the street is a mosque. Some days the road is crammed with cars and there are people everywhere, the men coming and going through the front door and the women, all in burkas, coming and going through the back. Women are only allowed in the mosque for funerals and on "women only" days. I think there have been at least ten funerals since the time we arrived. Once we pass the mosque, we are within a block of school. As we get close to the school, our car gets into the drop-off line. All cars have to be registered and have a card in the windshield with a number on it that corresponds with our children. As we approach the gate, an armed guard looks inside the car and the trunk, and then uses a big mirror to look under the car for explosives. We do this every time we enter and exit. As we go through the gate, we pass four more guards standing behind big barricades. All the guards are carrying automatic machine guns. Some of the guns date back to the Russian invasion. I'm always nervous that one will just go off spontaneously. When we reach the main building, our children are let out to go through the main door. In the afternoon, a guard on a walkie-talkie calls the children out, and they are walked to our car by another guard. Many of the Afghan children are part of important families and are escorted by bulletproof-vest-clad guards who walk on either side of the children. A friend of mine invited a little Afghan girl over to play one day, and it turned out she was one of the nieces of an important family; two armed guards stood in the yard with the little girl as she played all afternoon.

In the afternoon, after picking the children up, we sometimes will stop at the bakery where we can get fresh chocolate croissants and soda pop. It's one of the only places we can find sliced bread for the kids' lunches, too. After picking up our bread, we head home through the crazy traffic again. By the time we are heading back, the traffic can be twice as bad as when we left, so getting home sometimes takes twenty minutes to travel less than two kilometers. It's not a problem though because there are always wonderful sights to behold, more than I can really take in, actually. Today traffic was even slower, as there was a big herd of fat bottom sheep that needed to cross the road before the cars could move forward; with a herd of several hundred, it can take a while.

Personal Reflection

Traveling to school was always a highlight for me. During our time in Afghanistan, I was going several times a week to help at school with drama and music, and each and every trip was an adventure.

I loved the sights and sounds and smells of the busy streets. I was never allowed to walk on the street alone; but when I was safe within my car, I could take everything in as if I was out among the activities. I am intrigued with God's world, the diversity of people, culture, language, and landscape. When traveling in Kabul, I always felt as if I was in the middle of a copy of *National Geographic*. When I was a little girl, I never dreamed I would see the things I have seen or experience the places I have.

In our city there are many houses built into the side of the mountains scaling as far as the eye can see. Most of these homes are in ruins and barely keep families sheltered in the extreme temperatures of summer and winter. The glass in most of the windows has been shot out and broken by rockets. Entire walls and rooms are missing because they were destroyed during the fighting. Most homes have no running water. Twice a day small children, primarily girls, can be seen hauling old gas cans and plastic containers filled with water from the village well up and down the steep slopes of the mountains. The process can take hours and is exhausting. It was heartbreaking to watch, especially with the realization that this is all the life most of these children will ever experience.

Little girls in Afghanistan know little of playing and fun. Even into young adulthood, boys are encouraged to go outdoors and play; but it would never be acceptable for young girls to do the same. Little girls are not allowed out of the home after the age of about twelve unless they are going to school, and very few have that opportunity. Currently, the literacy rate for women in Afghanistan is less than ten percent and less than fifty percent for men.

In the past few years, more and more girls have been allowed to attend school. The increase is encouraging, especially considering that only ten years ago females were not allowed to be educated at all. Still, with less than ten percent actually attending school today, there is little hope for opportunities for the female population to advance. Even if young girls are allowed to go to school, most are only allowed to attend for a few years, as the family home needs them to care for the young and old within the household.

Each day as I sent my daughter off to school, I could hear the voices of young girls the same age as my daughter in the compounds next to our home doing laundry and cooking and washing dishes in the open areas of their property. There is a pecking order within each home, and the young girls are always at the bottom of the pile. By the time a young woman reaches puberty, it is most often time for the family to consider marriage for her. It is not uncommon for girls as young as twelve to be married off to husbands twenty or thirty years older.

A young girl who sat next to my daughter in school every day was a victim of this very custom. At the age of ten, her family married her off to a man in his sixties. Fortunately, a neighbor down the street from the man rescued her and then financially provided for her to attend school. Seeing this young girl in my daughter's class living a seemingly "normal" sixth grade life within the walls of school, yet knowing she had lived nothing remotely resembling the life of a sixth grader, left me feeling grateful and hopeless at the same time. My beautiful young daughter has lived in a family where she has had the opportunity to learn and experience that "the sky is the limit" as far as her potential goes. She has parents who would do anything to protect her from harm while trying to give her every opportunity to live a child's life. It is difficult to think that sitting right next to her is a young girl who was so abused and may never know or experience any of those things.

Although my daughter and her Afghan classmate shared the same classroom experience, their life experiences were extremely different. I am so grateful for the life my children have had, yet feel so helpless when thinking about all the suffering I observed as I walked out my life in Afghanistan. It was sometimes difficult to reconcile all I saw and experienced; I didn't know what to do with it all. During these moments, the Holy Spirit would remind me that it wasn't necessary for me to have the answers to all of the questions of why; I just had to be willing to give them to Him and to remember to stand in the gap for these people, to pray for God's protection and intervention in their lives. What hope can I offer? Only the Lord God Himself can bring about change in such a desperate place. My part is to be willing to go and do; and, if I can't, then my part is to pray.

Proverbs 22:6
Train up a child in the way he should go, and
when he is old he will not depart from it.

My first view of Afghanistan

The Hindu Kush mountains overlooking the city

Mountainside homes and communication towers

The open market on the Kabul River

Young boy selling balloons on a street near our home

A woman shopping in a sea of men

Young girls on their way to school

An Afghan family

Afghan Starbucks

A local meat market

Opium addicts outside a local shrine

Women selling sweets outside a local shrine

Roadside gas station

Donkey cart hauling produce to market

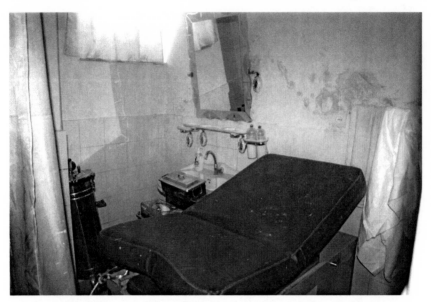

Birthing room in a community health center

**Shepherds taking their sheep and
straw down the mountain**

Hank's team playing soccer near the Darul Aman Palace

Laney taking in the mountaintop view near Istalif

Military vehicles heading toward Darul Aman Palace

**Laney and Hank entering their school as a
taxi is being checked for explosives**

Sign outside a local home

Shopping in Bush Bazaar with my friend Kate

Drying clothes on our rooftop

The view from the roof of our home

Letter 21 - Date Night in Kabul

Well, Monday was the six-week anniversary of our arrival and, to celebrate, Will and I decided to go out on our first date since arriving. We asked the other expats and got some good restaurant recommendations. We finally decided on a Lebanese restaurant on the other side of town. We made arrangements for the kids, made sure everyone's cell phones were charged up and had plenty of minutes of service on them, and made arrangements with the driver to leave when Will got home from work.

We left the house about 5:30 p.m. and it was already dark. Driving in this city after dark is a bit trickier than in the daytime. Traffic is usually bad and quite slow. There are usually checkpoints at night where we are stopped by the local police and have to show our papers. There is no good city lighting either, so it can be quite dark traveling from one place to another.

As we headed out, there was a driver change, and we were paired up with the newest driver in our compound. We knew we were headed for some trouble when we got into the car and as soon as we left the compound, the driver turned the radio on to a Bollywood/Dari party station and turned the music up so loud we couldn't carry on a conversation. Now this driver is new, and we didn't know him well, so we both hesitated to say anything to him, thinking he would get the hint as William and I were screaming at each other to talk. He never did. As we headed across town, the traffic was terrible; so it took us close to an hour to go about 15 kilometers. As we thought we were getting close to where the restaurant should be, we noticed that we had gone around the same round-about two different times and passed the same grocery store twice. At that point, the driver turned around to us and asked in broken English what the name of the restaurant was. We knew that wasn't a good sign. For the next half hour, we drove around in circles down dark back ally streets stopping every two blocks or so to ask people where the restaurant was. Now Afghans will never tell you they don't know something; they will just make it up when they don't know the answer to a question. Most of the people we asked had no clue what we were talking about and just sent us on more of a wild goose chase. William and I kept thinking, "Great; we're lost in Kabul in the dark with people with guns everywhere." After using the shark method (indefinite circling) for quite awhile, we finally arrived at the restaurant. Well, no wonder no one knew where it was; it was completely hidden behind a huge wall with barbed wire and a big metal gate. There was no sign, only a guard with a machine gun standing outside. At that point, we truly were trusting that we were actually going in for dinner and not going to be kidnapped along the way.

After going through two checkpoints and being frisked to make sure we weren't carrying weapons, even after the big sign that read, "NO WEAPONS ON PREMISES," we entered another world. I swear, when we walked in I felt like I had passed through the wardrobe into Narnia, or maybe it was more like falling down a hole into Wonderland. The restaurant was divided into two rooms; on one side there were glass tables with wicker chairs with full-sized sheep skins in them. There were also several lounge areas where groups of men were smoking hookah pipes. I totally expected to see the Cheshire cat staring back at me from one of the corners. Along the walls were sheets of rattan with Christmas lights woven into them. There were plastic flowers on the tables and birdcages with live birds along the tops of the walls.

On the other side of the glass partition there were tables and chairs made of ornate hand-carved mahogany wood with intricate carvings in the table-tops and along the table legs as well as the tops of the chairs. The chairs looked like something out of Genghis Khan's castle, a completely opposite motif from the beachfront scene on the other side of the glass wall. It was a bit much to take in all at once. We chose the Genghis Khan side and found a table in the center so we could watch all the interesting people coming and going. As I sat down, I noticed the walls were painted a bright orange, not a nice salmon or coral color, but a real orange like a Popsicle orange. On the wall above the table where we were sitting was a framed picture of an orange house cat. As I paid more attention, I realized there were lots of framed pictures of house cats. These pictures were not photographs of a person's pet, but a commercial type picture like something you would see in a calendar of "house cats;" you know, the ones that you can buy in the kiosks at the mall at Christmas. In the midst of the calendar cats, there was a large banner advertising Mercedes Benz (the kind you would find at a car dealership next to the obnoxious car salesman who you end up staring at while he pushes buttons on his calculator).

As we sat down, a waiter came to our table and asked us something in what I think was English but actually sounded like something Chewbacca would say. We decided to just try to order off the menu. We ended up ordering kabob and hummus. After putting in our order, the waiter came and brought us soup and two appetizers that he said were on the house. Thrilled, we dug in. I have to say that the food was some of the best food we have ever eaten. The hummus was wonderful. When we finished, we were given a piece of chocolate cake, also "on the house," and a cappuccino for me and jasmine tea for William. I'm not sure at all why those particular items showed up, but anyway... when we got ready to pay for the bill, we realized that "on the house" obviously doesn't mean the same thing here as it does at home, as our bill was $50 US.

Now, the food portion of our experience was wonderful; however, the atmosphere was a bit unusual; I mean, besides the aesthetics, which goes without saying. When we arrived, the restaurant was basically empty; but by the time we were getting our food, the place had exploded. There were close to fifty or sixty people in the two small rooms, mostly men; maybe three were women. There was a huge table on the Genghis Khan side filled with what looked like U.S. contract workers all talking loud and being obnoxious. On the seaside-hut side, there were two big groups of Afghan and Lebanese men smoking hookahs and eating kabob. Both groups looked like there were a few stories to tell among them. As we ate, more and more groups of men came in, standing around waiting for a table. At one point I looked up and saw our driver standing with one of the groups. He walked in and sat down behind us and started reading a magazine, staring over the top of it at me. Now those of you who don't have drivers might not know that it's a big time "no, no" for a driver to leave the car, especially in Kabul, and it's certainly not okay to come into an establishment and stand behind your employer and stare at his wife!

By the time we finished our chocolate cake and paid for our "on the house" food, the room was full of high profile men and hookah smoke. We know the other clients in the restaurant were high profile people, even if it was only in their minds, because there were twenty-plus guards standing in the road with machine guns guarding their hundred thousand dollar vehicles when we walked to our car.

Our trip home was much faster than our trip out, for which we were both very thankful. There were no checkpoints or bad traffic jams, though we had to listen to yet another episode of Dari Bandstand on max volume. By the time we got home, we decided that maybe for the next anniversary celebration we would just stay home and pop some popcorn and eat chocolate cake made in our own kitchen.

Just in case you're wondering, our driver no longer works for our NGO. I guess there were some other problems building, and leaving the car in the middle of Ghetto-Ville to come in and stare at us during dinner was the last straw!

Personal Reflection

When I think about this story, it still brings a smile to my face. In some weird way, it kind of sums up our life together - one big adventure! Our date that night was funny, sweet, refreshing, adventurous, and a bit unnerving at times; but the whole time, God protected and provided for us! We stepped out of the norm, and God was with us every step of the way! I am so grateful that God has given me the life He has; I wouldn't trade it for anything! I have never been bored, that is for sure!

This kind of adventure is what God desires for us all! He desires that each day with Him is an adventure in faith. Whether we go across the street or around the world, God wants us to know that He desires life to be funny, sweet, refreshing, challenging and always an adventure. God doesn't want us to live a mundane life of lack, routine or boredom. Ask Him each day what kind of an adventure He has in store for you, then step out of your safety zone and partner with Him in the great adventures of life. I promise He has something waiting in the wings for you – take a chance and accept it!

Psalm 91:1-2
He who dwells in the secret place of the Most High shall abide under the shadow of the Almighty. I will say of the Lord, "He is my refuge and my fortress; My God, in Him I will trust."

Letter 22 - We Are Going to a Wedding

Will and I were invited to a wedding this week. The son of one of the doctors who works with William at the hospital is getting married and our family has been asked to attend. It's a great honor to be invited to a national's wedding; so, of course, we accepted. There is really a benefit for both sides. The doctor will be greatly admired and appreciated for having foreigners attend the wedding of his son; and it will be a great National Geographic *moment for my kids, as well as great blog material for me.*

Now, even though typically guests are formally invited only a few days in advance, there are still some cultural must do's that have to happen. First and foremost is shopping for wedding clothes.

Yesterday I asked my housemate, Kate, to go along with me to the local "mall" to shop for wedding outfits for Laney and me. Kate and I headed out with our driver to the center of town to a huge seven-story structure that houses all the "local" shops for clothes for the important events in Afghans' lives. After crossing two busy streets on foot, dodging cars, carts, buses, donkeys, and sheep, and then walking through three inches of sewer sludge from the jewie (open sewer trenches along the main roads) with a revolting smell, we finally made our way into the building. By the time we looked up, we realized that we had caused quite a stir amongst the locals, being the only foreigners there. This is the week before Eid, a huge Muslim holiday, so the entire city of Kabul was out shopping for new outfits. All of them had stopped dead in their tracks to stare at the two white ladies hopping through the sewer.

Kate and I navigated a couple floors of items, working our way through fabric, coats, and children's clothes, making it to the third floor where the "party" frocks are. Now please picture two American women who do not know Dari, pushing and shoving their way through hijab- and burka-clad groups of women, trying to find appropriate outfits for an Afghan event. Each store is about ten feet by ten feet, packed floor to ceiling with clothes. All along the walls are crazy mannequins dressed in the outfits that we could choose from. There are no dressing rooms and no real sizes marked on anything, so we had to look at each and every piece of clothing to try to decide if it would fit or not. After finding a piece that we thought might work, we had to push and shove our way to the counter to try to negotiate a price. Now, most storeowners do not speak English, and we don't speak Dari, so we used our phone calculators to show the owner how much we were willing to pay. Sometimes we just had to walk away if a price could not be agreed upon. Now, there is a stupid thing that happens to foreigners who bargain…the more we haggle, the more a dollar makes a difference; when we finally walk away, we realize that we lost the bargain over some crazy small amount like fifty cents or a dollar; but we're so mad that he wouldn't budge, that we move on to

146

the next store and start the whole process over... FOR A DOLLAR! REALLY? It's more about the game than it is the amount, and dadgum, I'm going to win! It's ridiculous, actually.

I think it's important for you to understand that Afghans know how to party; don't let the burka fool you. Underneath the sea of blue, each woman at a wedding is dressed in head-to-toe "bling." Think about the wildest prom or pageant dress you can imagine and multiply it by ten. Feathers, ruffles, sequins, mirrors, ribbon, tulle, flowers and it's all on the same dress. Some dresses are so heavy with sequins, I can't even lift them. Most of the styles are very Western with tiny spaghetti straps or even strapless. In this culture, sleeveless is inappropriate, so each shopkeeper sells a variety of skintight long-sleeved shirts to match the gowns that the ladies wear under the Victoria's Secret style dresses. Of course, that all seems a bit silly to me when the men and women party in separate rooms. Along with the over-the-top dresses, each woman has her hair piled high up on her head with more sequins. Most are wearing all the jewelry they own, and enough makeup to keep MAC cosmetics in business for a year. "My big fat Greek wedding" has nothing on an Afghan wedding. Now, I'm a good sport and up for the party attire as much as the next gal, but this is a bit much even for me. The hunt for an understated but bedazzled outfit was a challenge for this girl, as well as for my twelve-year-old daughter.

After about an hour, we looked up and realized that there was a group of about ten burka-clad women who were following Kate and me from store to store just so they could stare at us. At one point, I turned my head to meet a woman six inches from my face, unblinking, watching me. It's not rude to stare in this culture, unless you are a foreigner staring at them! So in most cases, we just had to put up with it. Kate and I kept telling ourselves that it's really a compliment. It is fun though, to just talk out loud to each other about the experience, as neither group understands the other's language. I guarantee, the Afghan women were doing the same.

After two hours of hunting, pushing, sorting, and bargaining, we finally decided on outfits for both Laney and me. We then made our way down four floors to the basement to hunt for our bling-embellished shoes to match. I really should make this a separate letter because it was like stepping into another experience altogether; but for the sake of your time and mine, I won't. The summary is that there are thousands of shoes lining the walls stacked in the hall and doorways. Each shop has a little plastic stool to sit on if you want to try on a shoe. Trying on a shoe is not as easy as it may seem, though. Some stores are no bigger than a closet and I had to sit down and take off my shoe and sock while still keeping my chadar on. I had to be very modest and not show too much leg, and I had to juggle all my packages in my lap while a crowd of five to ten people stood around and watched me. If the store didn't have my size, which is likely because the only ones they have are the ones sitting out, and every shoe that was out looks to be about a 4, the shopkeeper will send a runner to other stores to find you another. It doesn't matter what size they bring back. Even if I'm a 6 and the shoe they brought is a 10, I had to try it on and prove to them that it does or doesn't fit. If my heel was hanging off the back or even if there were three inches of shoe behind my heel, the shopkeeper would try to convince me that it's perfect. After another hour of hunting, we finally decided on a low heeled, modestly embellished, sandal. Now like the dresses, I am all about looking fashionable and cute; but the normal 5-inch heel, Bollywood style shoe that most women wear here was just not going to make the cut for me or my twelve-year-old daughter. I mean, come on, people, it's not like there are sidewalks and nice cars that drive you up to the door of an event. Most often, you have to walk on broken ground across several streets and jump a jewie before you walk into the door. I am not going to do that in 5-inch heels. Call me a party- pooper if you want!

So after three hours of "the hunt," Kate and I made it back into the sunshine only to discover that our driver was nowhere to be found, and we were standing in a sea of several hundred men selling their wares on the sidewalk. After about ten minutes, our driver found us in the crowd; not too hard for him, as we were the only white women

ANYWHERE. Our driver led us through the crowd down the street and around the corner to where the van was parked. At this point, he was very frustrated with us as he missed lunch and was late for prayers. He drove like a NASCAR driver all the way home as fast as he could, jumped out of the car, and ran to his chowkidar (guard) house to pray. Later that day, when I went to pick the kids up from school, I stopped at the French bakery and got him a chocolate croissant. That seemed to make everything okay, though he might not be so willing to take us shopping next time!

Personal Reflection

This experience—shopping for our wedding clothes—was some of the most fun I had while in Kabul. My housemate and I were out shopping by ourselves, laughing and having the time of our lives while mixing with the locals. We got to experience, firsthand, how the women of Afghanistan shop for special events and see a side of the culture that is rarely witnessed by foreigners. That day in the "mall," I saw the most women in one place while living in the country. It must have been one of the only places their husbands allow them to go alone. Shopping that day in the local market brought a feeling of independence that is rare in this place. Maybe that is why it was so popular with the locals as well. It was a blast to be the only one of our kind in a mix of hundreds, conversing and going about our business in our own little world, while in the throng of others. Of course, I shudder to think what bad things could have happened in that situation, alone in an Afghan market unable to speak the language and without a male escort. Maybe Kate and I were a bit risky that day going out on our own; but, man, was it fun!

Nehemiah 8:10
For this day is holy to our Lord. Do not sorrow,
for the joy of the Lord is your strength.

Letter 23 - Movie Star for a Day

Well, we made it, our first Afghan wedding. It was a very nice evening all in all, even though I felt bad for the bride and groom, as I think their foreign guests upstaged their evening a few times. Not because we wanted to, quite the opposite. If we could have blended in, it would have been so much nicer.

The wedding officially started at 5:00 p.m.; however, that just means we don't show up until two hours later. After an afternoon of nails, hair, and makeup, our curious foreign group showed up to the Kabul Dubai Wedding Hall right on time at 7:00 p.m.

Contrary to what I said earlier about not wearing high heels, I broke my own rule and brought out the red pumps. I just couldn't let all those beautiful ladies show me up by sporting such high fashion in such a harsh environment. So, after arriving and navigating through gravel and jewies (open sewers) and traffic, we made it into the halls – each person to their respective sides, please (men in one hall, women and children in the other)!

As our small group of women entered the hall, we were greeted by the groom's mother. She took us around the hall, full of five hundred plus women and children. After about an hour of introductions and kisses, we were taken to our table. Laney was quite the entertainment to the young girls attending the wedding. At one point, two little girls arranged their chairs right behind Laney, so they could watch her through the night. The other ladies at our table were midwives whom we had met before and who speak fairly good English; so it was easier to have conversations, though it really wasn't possible to hear them talk most of the time over the crazy loud music.

After some time, the bride and groom were brought into the hall followed by many of the women dancing behind them. The groom was the only male in the building. The bride and groom were taken to a stage with huge king and queen type chairs where they sat and oversaw the activities There was a time of pictures with the guests; and before we knew it our group of four was asked to go onto the stage and have our pictures taken with the bride and groom. The bride is never allowed to smile during the wedding and, in some village weddings, they are expected to cry and wail. If a bride smiles and acts happy, she brings dishonor to her family. She must act sad to be leaving. The groom, on the other hand, is allowed to smile and act happy as he has gained a prized possession. After way more pictures than I was comfortable with, we were allowed to go back to our seats.

We had not been back in our seats but for a few minutes when suddenly there was a group of women standing behind us speaking in Dari and motioning us to move toward the front. After one of the ladies at our table so graciously interpreted for us what was going on, we found ourselves being pushed to the front of the room to the dance floor where we were expected to go out and dance for the bride and groom ALONE! After some begging and pleading, we did talk one other lady into going out with us, so we would at least know what to do. At one point, I looked up and saw the groom laughing - I hoped that was a good sign. The whole thing was incredibly awkward. I have never danced Bollywood style before and certainly not with four-inch heels while being videoed (for the long winter night's entertainment of the groom's family, I'm sure).

After our dance, we were led back to our seats to wait for dinner. I never fully relaxed though, not knowing what else I might be asked to do. After about an hour's wait, dinner finally arrived by way of running waiters carrying large trays. As they approached the table, they would swing the trays around in a circle and plop them down on the table. A woman would then literally throw the trays into their respective spots. Each table was given a roasted chicken, five kinds of rice, about 15 lamb kabobs, a plate of cut cucumbers, a plate of spiced cauliflower, an Afghan dish of mantu, cardamom pudding, rose water pudding, and plates of apples and bananas. It was absolutely a miracle *that all the food even fit on the table, and a bigger miracle that it was all eaten by the end of the evening. After our food was on our table, a waiter came by pushing a shopping cart with cans of pop that were stacked in groups of twelve with shrink wrap around them. Each table got a package of mixed flavors. I'm sorry to report that there was no Diet Coke, however; only Mountain Dew and orange soda... go figure.*

After our food was gone, we were free to go and thank our host and take our leave. At this point, we had been in the wedding hall for three hours, and Laney was about to fall over from exhaustion.

Afghan weddings are most certainly a huge affair. Most couples go into significant debt to pay off the evening. To have a wedding in these big halls and feed upward of 1,000 people, the evening can end up costing up to $10,000 US dollars. This is a lot of money in this country; money that most families do not have. I asked a Muslim friend about this whole crazy upside down thing, and he told me that the Koran teaches just the opposite: that a wedding should be very low key affair, just a small ceremony where each family exchanges a drink and a meal. These large ceremonies are a cultural thing that I believe has been birthed out of many years of war and sadness. A wedding is one of the only events in this culture that people truly get excited about. It's the only time people get to freely go out and "party," socializing with their peers and enjoying good food and company. It's just so sad that it's also the one thing that can put a family into financial ruin for years to come.

As a family, we were very honored and excited to attend such a cultural event, but I can honestly say that one was enough.

Personal Reflection

Attending an Afghan wedding as a foreigner is a huge honor and a once-in-a-lifetime event. I felt a bit like the foreigner on parade, though a guest. I don't know if we were invited because of our relationship with the groom's father or if it was just an opportunity for the family to show off their "white" friends. I can see the scene for years to come as the family sits on cold winter nights, year after year, watching the video of the crazy Americans at their wedding. No matter what the reason, I was grateful for the experience. There is so much sadness in this country that it was a real treat to see some of the happier moments of the culture.

Luke 14:8
"When someone invites you to a wedding feast, do not take the place of honor, for a person more distinguished than you may have been invited. (New International Version)

CHAPTER 7 – Unexpected Blessings

Deuteronomy 28:1-3

Now it shall come to pass, if you diligently obey the voice of the Lord your God, to observe carefully all His commandments which I command you today, that the Lord your God will set you high above all nations of the earth. And all these blessings shall come upon you and overtake you, because you obey the voice of the Lord your God: Blessed shall you be in the city, and blessed shall you be in the country.

Letter 24 - A Land of Heartache

I'm having a hard time putting words to page about my latest experience here in this country. I don't know how to transfer feelings of pain, hopelessness, and grief into a medium that does it justice. I wish somehow I could help you see, hear, and touch the precious people that I have been honored to meet this week.

Two days ago, our family had the profound honor and privilege to be a part of a relief distribution here in Kabul. We were able to partner with an organization that gave away large sacks of food and a blanket to each family living in an IDP (internally displaced person) camp. Each family living in this camp is there because their homes and families have been destroyed by war. Most are from the Helmand province and are Pashtun and have lost everything because of the war.

As we entered the camp, we were met by the village leaders and were asked to share some tea before starting the distribution. There were hundreds of men in attendance and no women besides Laney, Kate, and me. It was a great honor and very humbling to sit surrounded by the leaders of this community. These men, all who held places of authority in their homelands, were now trying to hold on to their dignity as they had no choice but to receive help from foreigners. The head elder of the community, the equivalent of a mayor in our culture, sat with us, and as he drank his tea, told us of the horrors he had lived through. In order to take care of his family, he now picks up trash all day.

As we prepared to pass out the blankets and food, dozens of men came up to us and showed us their papers, laminated documents with personal information along with pictures of family members who had been killed in the war. There was not a man in the camp who did not have multiple pictures on his sheet. One gentleman, who appeared to be in his seventies, approached to tell us his story. As he spoke through an interpreter, this gentleman told us of his wife and family who had been killed by a bomb. Tears ran down his cheeks as he spoke of his wife, who he said he loved very much. This man's story was just the first of many others we heard this day - story after story of tragic heartache and loss.

The head of each family was issued a number that was then traded for the blanket and food. As I watched the men go past me to receive their things, I realized that many of the men were actually just young boys, some no older than six or seven. These small boys had to carry the fifty-pound bag of food on their backs; quite a load for such small shoulders, a load that was literally much bigger than they were equipped to carry. I realized that these small boys were in line because there were no other men left in their families. These small boys now carried the responsibility of providing for their mothers and siblings.

The families in this camp live in mud huts with no running water or electricity. Most families arrived here after days of travel with only the clothes on their backs. Most owned land and homes and herds of cattle or sheep where they came from and are now trying to live with no means to support themselves. The children are hungry and dirty and cold. Most of the children we saw had no shoes or coats, even though it gets below freezing each night during this time of year. There is only one well for the entire community of 3,000-plus people. There is no sewage system or indoor plumbing of any kind. Most homes have no stoves or supplies, no beds, no blankets, and no extra clothing.

As we traveled through the village, we were taken to family after family who had someone sick, injured, or dying. One little girl, about the age of 11, had lost her arm to a bomb. Another young mother had lost four of her seven children, her husband, sister and brother-in-law when a bomb hit her community; she herself had been injured when a wall fell onto her leg, breaking it just above the ankle. This young mother told me she had no will to live and wanted to die as she woke each day trying to figure out how to provide for her three other children when she couldn't walk and had no husband or home. Her two small babies were playing in the trash as we spoke.

As you can imagine, it was very difficult to stay focused on what I needed to do while actually wanting to just sit down and cry with each of these families. I had nothing to offer them except a bit of warmth and enough food to last them a couple of weeks.

As I walked through this little village of heartache, I couldn't help but wonder - why them and not me? Why do I get to go home and sleep in a warm bed, build a fire, and eat until I am full? Why do my children live and theirs die? Why can I wake up each day with hope for my future and opportunity for my family? These precious people have done nothing to bring these hardships on themselves. Each and every one of them wants the same things I do and, yet, here they are living in complete poverty and hopelessness. I realized as I looked around that, without a mild winter, many of them would not be here in the spring.

As I contemplated the question of why them and not me, I realized I am where I am, not because of any doing of myself, but because of the choices and decisions that others before me have made. Just like these people I met. They are in this horrible place because of the choices of others. Good and bad - that's really what it all comes down to. We are where we are because of those who have gone before us, and our choices will directly affect those who go after us. Don't misunderstand me; we must take responsibility for our own choices, and they, too, directly affect where we end up. But, I have the privileges and provisions I do because my home country was fought for and established on principles based on truth: respect for life and honor to Him who created us; sacrifices made generations before me giving me the liberty I live in; choices made by my parents and grandparents that have given me knowledge, truth, and experience; choices that have filled me with hope and opportunity. The choices that I am now making on a daily basis will also affect generations to come. These precious people are now experiencing heartache because of the choices of those who have gone before them, and their choices will now directly affect their generations to come after them. Without the knowledge of truth and life, the cycle of death and destruction will continue to go on and on.

I prayed for these people as I walked through the streets of hopelessness. I prayed that God would provide for them, that their babies would live, and that their country would find peace. I prayed that evil would disperse from that place and that somehow these people would find hope, truth, and life. I am one person with little resources for a need like this; however, I house a truth in my heart that is bigger than this heartache. If my heart is broken for these precious people, I know the heart of God is more so. Though it was hard, I am thankful for the experience to be reminded that my world is so much bigger than me and mine, and I have a responsibility to do what I can to give love and comfort where I can while still knowing that God is bigger than even this.

Personal Reflection

God's heart is broken for the people of this world. These people suffering in the IDP camp are His creation. God's heart is broken for injustices in Afghanistan and many other places; but He needs us, His body, to do something about it. We, the body of Christ, are the hands and feet of Jesus; we are the ones who can feed a hungry child, or clothe a widow or give medicine to the sick and weak and fragile. We are the ones who can give a cup of cool water or a blanket for warmth. I was so honored to be a part of an organization doing something to help these people; but it wasn't enough, and the resources we had would only last a few weeks. What happens after that? Where will the people get their food then? How will their children live to be adults? How can the people's dignity and honor be restored? These are difficult questions, ones without answers. I know that the answer for these people is Jesus Himself, but I also know that Jesus desires us to show a hurting world His character by loving and supporting them.

There were many nights as I lay in my warm bed through the winter in Kabul that I thought of the people in the IDP camp. I prayed that God would protect them and provide for them. I prayed that God would reveal Himself to them and give them a hope and a purpose. As I prayed for these people, I also thanked God for the opportunities my children and I have had because of the choices of those who have gone before us. I thanked Him for my warm bed and food to eat. I thanked Him for His provision and His truth, and I prayed that the people in the IDP camp would make it through another winter.

Matthew 25:34-40

Then the King will say to those on His right hand, 'Come, you blessed of My Father, inherit the kingdom prepared for you from the foundation of the world: for I was hungry and you gave Me food; I was thirsty and you gave Me drink; I was a stranger and you took Me in; I was naked and you clothed Me; I was sick and you visited Me; I was in prison and you came to Me.' Then the righteous will answer Him, saying, 'Lord, when did we see You hungry and feed You, or thirsty and give You drink? When did we see You a stranger and take You in, or naked and clothe You? Or when did we see You sick, or in prison, and come to You?' And the King will answer and say to them, 'Assuredly, I say to you, inasmuch as you did it to one of the least of these My brethren, you did it to Me.'

Letter 25 - Our Trip to Istalif

This week is Eid, a very important Muslim holiday. Equivalent in some ways to our Christmas holiday, Eid is the celebration to honor the near sacrifice of Abraham's son, an important prophet to Muslims. For Muslims, this holiday is marked by the slaughter of a lamb or goat and then three days of feasting and visiting friends and relatives. Because of the observance of this holiday, the kids' school was closed all week. As a family, we felt that this time would be a good opportunity to get out of the city and visit the beautiful mountain village of Istalif.

We headed out Monday morning and drove about two hours outside the city. We spent an hour on the pavement of the highway and then another hour on the winding dirt roads climbing up into the mountains. The farther we drove, the more beautiful the landscape became. The air was clearer and the sky brighter. As we wound up tiny dirt roads, only inches at times from the houses that lined the edge of the mountains, we took in the beautiful view of a rough and rugged rock landscape. After about an hour on the dirt road, we found ourselves at the end of where a car could pass. I say this with hesitation because I couldn't believe that for nearly the last half hour a car could pass through the terrain that we did. At the end of the road sat a small village overlooking the river that passes through the mountains. We left the car, put on our backpacks, and headed out for a half-hour hike up the riverbed to where our lodge sat nestled in a crook of the mountains. We were told that in the spring, the river runs so high and fast that the half-hour walk turns into an hour or an hour and a half, as people must navigate the terraced landscape of the mountainside instead of walking up the almost dry riverbed, as we did.

After a beautiful hike up the river, jumping rocks and dodging donkeys, we arrived at the lodge. We only lost one bag into the river. Fortunately, most of what was in the bag was enclosed in plastic, so not much harm done, except to Hank, as he had to thaw out his legs after slipping into the freezing water to retrieve the bag.

The little village that sits in these beautiful mountains has been untouched by time or war. There are no cars in the area and everything must be hauled in by hand or donkey. Most of the families in the area are farmers and herders of sheep and goats. The harsh mountains are hand terraced up the sides where crops are planted in the spring and used to feed the village and livestock through the winters. As we hiked the mountains and saw the terraced fields firsthand, we were amazed; we could barely stand on the steep grade of the mountain let alone haul dirt and rocks and tend a field. No wonder the average age of an

Afghan man is 55 in this country. If they don't die of war, starvation, or sickness, they work themselves to death.

Our second day in Istalif, we climbed the mountain that faced our lodge. It took us about an hour to scale the side. Several times we wondered if we should stop, as it was so high and rugged. As we climbed, I couldn't help but reflect on a book I have read several times, "Hinds Feet on High Places." The pages of this book are a metaphor of life and the struggles we face daily, a spiritual story of the guidance and help we can receive from God when we allow it. The story came alive to me as I put one foot in front of another pushing toward the top. As I struggled to push myself in this challenge, there were herds of goats and sheep that literally leapt past me navigating the rocks and terrain as if they were on flat ground, their tiny hooves never slipping or struggling as they pushed forward to the green grazing grounds at the higher elevations. As the herds made their climb, they never lost sight of their shepherd, staying always within the range of his voice. The herds would wander and scatter at times, but it only took one whistle of the shepherd to get them back on track. They seemed so free and content as the only responsibility they had was to follow the voice and leading of their shepherd, knowing that he would lead them to all the provision they would need.

On the third morning of our stay, I woke to the sound of the shepherd herding the sheep once again up the mountain. I sat at my window and watched the process, amazed at how simplistic and beautiful the metaphor was for me. As I watched the shepherd lead his flock up the mountain, I was reminded of the story of another shepherd; his name was David. David walked mountains much like the ones I was then looking at. I could imagine him going out early in the morning every day and not returning until dark, spending his days alone with only sheep to keep him company. David must have known every crevice and bend in every inch of the mountains his sheep walked. He spent his days protecting his herds, looking out for them, providing for them day after day, year after year. I'm sure as *the days and years passed he never imagined where his future would take him. A shepherd boy that ended up a king!*

As I thought of this story, I couldn't help but wonder what the little boys and girls of this forgotten land could grow up to be. What mighty things could they accomplish? If only they knew what wonders lay beyond their mountains; if only they could know the truth.

As I gazed across this amazing landscape, I was humbled and so grateful to be where I was. Who would have thought this little Texas girl would someday be looking at the beauty and wonder of this forgotten land? How blessed I am.

Our trip away was a wonderful break from the crazy, dusty, confined life of the city. It gave us new perspective and renewed vision for our time here. We spent precious moments with our children enjoying the wonder of creation and the beauty of each other. In a way, we experienced stepping back in time, enjoying life without the clutter of noise, stuff, and schedules. It was a treat indeed.

Personal Reflections

Istalif is one of the few places in Afghanistan that has not been as devastated and destroyed as the rest of the country. The landscape is breathtaking, rugged, and harsh. The lodge we stayed in was simple and clean. We slept on toshaks (long cushions used as furniture) and warmed ourselves under a sandalese (a low table covered with a heavy tablecloth with a small fire or heat-lamp underneath). We ate Afghan food and drank tea, read books, played games and hiked along the river and up the mountains.

It's hard to imagine that people in this region are born, live and die while never leaving the small mountain village of Istalif. What a simple and uncomplicated life. I wondered, though, if the small children tending the flocks ever looked to the summit of the mountains and imagined what lies beyond them. I wondered if they even know that their country is at war, that people are starving and desperate. Here in this little village, the people grow their own food in gardens and raise goats and sheep for meat and wool. There is a beautiful river and ample electricity due to an hydroelectric wheel put in by an NGO. There is little need for the outside world. I wonder if the people look at the star-filled skies of their world and wonder about their Creator? Even in this quiet little village with little knowledge of what horrors lie beyond their mountains, the people need a Savior. God placed inside of us all a need to fill a void that only He can fill. We were all born with the innate understanding that we came from something and we should seek that "something." Islam is strong, even in this quiet village. Women veil and carry the brunt of the load of life while the men smoke their hookahs and solve the problems of village life. It's woven into every fabric of life and will not unravel easily. Here in this quiet sleepy village, I fear that "truth" is harder to convey because there is little need for change. Satan understands that by keeping people ignorant and isolated, there is little need for or opportunity to seek out anything other than his agenda. Sound familiar? The Taliban did the same thing when they invaded Afghanistan in the early 1990's.

When the Taliban took over Afghanistan, they quickly removed all the forms of communication that Afghans had with the outside world. All the televisions, radios, and phones were confiscated. Even the books were taken and burned. The Taliban took all reminders of history and culture, stating that it bred immoral behavior. Afghans were forbidden to travel outside the country, and schools were shut down except for the Islamic schools for boys. The educated people of the country, especially the women, were stripped of their jobs and at times, even their lives. The Taliban controlled all the information coming in and going out of the country. People were kept in the dark about what was going on outside of their borders and all the information that could enrich or enlarge their lives.

The harshest restrictions were put on women. Women were literally locked inside their homes. The windows were painted black so no one could see in or out. They were forbidden to be on the streets or outside of their courtyards; they were not allowed to go to school or work. During this time, women were forbidden to wear makeup or adorn themselves in any way. Some women, who dared to wear nail polish, were made examples by having their fingers cut off.

Two of the biggest ways that Satan oppresses people is through ignorance and fear. If people are not able to think for themselves and fear doing so because of impending punishment or death, they become easy to control. If kept in this state long enough, they become like robots, believing and reacting to everything their controllers tell them. For the past ten years, Afghanistan has been in a type of awakening, becoming aware for the first time in this generation of the good and bad of life outside. Unfortunately, because of the evil that has prevailed within the borders of this land, more bad than good has gotten in. In this sleepy town of Istalif, beautiful and backward, untouched by outside influences, life goes on as it always has, with little need for change, protected by the mountains, isolated by its location, simple and beautiful but still in need of a Savior.

Psalm 23:1-2
The Lord is my shepherd; I shall not want. He makes me to lie down in green pastures; He leads me beside the still waters.

Letter 26 - A Life of Thanksgiving

This week, as we work towards the holiday of Thanksgiving, I am realizing that it means more to me this year than any year in the past that I can remember. There are so many things for which I am reminded to be thankful. The holiday itself helps us remember the sacrifices made hundreds of years ago. Think about those pilgrims crossing the sea to a new land in search of religious tolerance and independence. Those brave men and women had no idea what they were headed for, the hardships that would ensue; they were just in search of a better place for themselves and their families. I cannot imagine the courage it must have taken to leave everything behind knowing they would never see their loved ones or homeland again. Because of the sacrifices of these families, we have America today. I am so grateful for what those men and women did for us. After living for a few months in a country where independence and freedoms are defined differently than I am used to, I appreciate so much more what I have back home and what was done for us as a nation. What an amazing heritage we have. I am discouraged, at times, at how far we have come from the founding principles of the nation. I am saddened to think about what those men and women who sacrificed for us would think if they saw some of the attitudes and arrogance our culture displays today. We have strayed quite far from those founding principles of our forefathers. We have so much for which to be grateful.

This week, three of our children had birthdays; it was the first time in 23 years we have not all been together to celebrate those days. I found myself battling sadness and loneliness a bit. As I reflected, though, on all we have and how well God has taken care of us, my heart felt like it would burst with gratitude. As I sit in my warm room next to my wood-burning stove, I think of the precious people at the IDP camp without heat and food and warm clothes. I have enough food to eat, I am warm and clothed; my children are educated. My husband has steady work. I am not beaten or locked inside my house. I can read and write. I can drive and go where I want (at home, that is). I can worship however I choose. I live with peace in my heart and a knowing that my destiny is secure. Grateful, grateful, grateful! I should wake up each and every day and start the day with "thank you."

So many times in my life in America I would find myself so caught up in schedules and expectations that it was hard to see what I had. I am so thankful for the opportunity to simplify and slow down enough to see all the good in what I do have. I am thankful for the contrast and contradictions I am experiencing, for they all direct me to gratitude. I am thankful for the opportunity to live outside myself and see things bigger and even greater than I could imagine, both good and bad. I am grateful for the opportunity to feel uncomfortable and stretched, as it helps me focus on what is important and Who is really in control. I am thankful! I have realized, as well, that I had all the same opportunities before to experience this kind of gratitude; I just rarely took advantage of them. It takes determination and a conscious act of my will to be grateful in abundance. That's a sad revelation for me. I am determined, now more than ever, to live a life of gratitude no matter where my feet walk and head lies. I want to live with a determination to find a list of things each and every day for which to be thankful. I want to be proactive about gratitude, not only for my own heart, but so that I can be aware of the needs of those around me. I want to always be in situations where the blessings in my life can spill over into others. I am determined to live a life of thankfulness!

Personal Reflection

Celebrating an American holiday while living in a foreign country was a sweet experience. A group of about fifty people from different countries got together to give thanks to our God and Creator. It was wonderful to share such a special day with Europeans, Africans, and Asians; what a colorful and diverse group we were. The common denominator of getting together wasn't so much an American holiday; it was the opportunity to share a common belief in Jesus Christ and what was done and given to us through Him; we all wanted to take time to thank Him.

We had a potluck dinner with all the Thanksgiving staples: mashed potatoes, yams, green beans, stuffing, and, of course, an elephant chicken. An "elephant chicken" is what the Afghans call turkey. There are no turkeys in Afghanistan, so when turkey is flown into the country for our American holidays, the closest reference for the Afghans is a chicken that is very, very large like an elephant. It was fun to share our American traditions and food with our Afghan staff. I think they think we are a bit backwards in some things; but they could all be found sitting in the wings of the event, listening and observing a love and thankfulness we had for each other and our Lord. It was a very special day; I don't think I will ever look at Thanksgiving quite the same way again.

Living in a community with so many diverse cultures, backgrounds and beliefs proved to be one of the many gifts this trip gave me, though at times it was one of the most challenging aspects of the journey. Human nature is the same no matter what language is spoken. We are all at our core selfish, prideful, insecure and rough around the edges. Living in community under the best of circumstances can be challenging; but add in security threats, lack of heat, water and electricity, spiritual oppression and social differences, and it could be a set-up for disaster. I think one of the most interesting dynamics I witnessed while living in such diversity is what I call "the changing of the guards." In Afghanistan there is a lot of coming and going in the expat community. Circumstances change quickly, and there is a huge need for flexibility and adjustments. The average lifespan of an expat in Afghanistan is about two years, though there are a few who have been there ten or more. With such a high degree of turnover, there is a constant mix of the "old" and the "new" as people are coming and going and navigating through their own set of unique circumstances. With this situation comes a lot of opportunity for the "newcomers" bringing in their new ideas and fresh passion to step on some toes of the "old timers." There is an interesting mix of conversations and scenarios surrounding the tried and true approaches and the new and fresh ones.

As the new ones come in, they are excited about the potential and possibilities of change and revelation, and at the same time the older ones are frustrated and worn down with the revelation that only God brings change. Often hearts are hard and wounded, and on the surface there is little fruit to see for the years of sacrifice and labor. Neither perspective is wrong, and both have great value in the big picture. Often the new ones bring encouragement and life to the community while the old ones bring stability and wisdom. It's actually a beautiful dance to watch and be a part of, and, if done right, brings incredible momentum and potential to the ever-changing landscape of life in Afghanistan.

The flip side of the coin is that with the entire turnover there is always an opportunity for fresh and meaningful relationships that refine and encourage and challenge. The beautiful things I learned from my fellow expats will forever help me to see life differently and encourage me to see new perspectives and ways of thinking.

Some of the sweetest times spent together as a community was at our weekly church services. With the diverse cultures, languages, and religious backgrounds there is a huge risk for division and on occasion that did occur, but for the most part, the simple denominator that brought us together each week was Jesus. Our worship and fellowship was very simplistic and real. We all volunteered for the many responsibilities like security, worship, and snacks, and often had opportunities to share about our victories and our heartaches. We prayed for each other and hugged each other and sometimes pushed and challenged each other as we slipped into self-pity and pride. There was a level of trust and transparency with each other that I have rarely witnessed in the West. Life in a war zone will teach you to let go of pretense and just be real; if you are going to share a bomb shelter together, you'd best cut to the chase and learn to love through the differences. We didn't need to argue about the different doctrines or customs; we simply thanked and worshiped our Father and His Son Who had brought us all together in the first place. I especially appreciated this element for our children who had the opportunity to experience a small community of believers working and living together to honor and serve Jesus. There was no big screen TV or dance club lighting, no gimmicks, no giveaways, no games, no stage show or hype, though there is a place for all of that in certain settings and cultures. I was grateful for the opportunity to share a different way of doing things with my children that, hopefully, will help shape their ideas of what is really important to them and their worship.

1 Thessalonians 5:18

In everything give thanks; for this is the will of God in Christ Jesus for you.

Letter 27 - My Shift in the NICU

Today I had the privilege of doing something I never thought I would do while living here in this country. I got to spend a few hours "kangaroo holding" (skin to skin) a little preemie baby because her Afghan mother couldn't because she was too sick.

We have a friend who is a NICU (neonatal intensive care unit) nurse working here in the only hospital where they can take care of babies born prematurely. Five weeks ago, a set of twin girls were born. One was a lot bigger and healthier than the other and was able to go home after a few short weeks. The sister ended up having to have bowel surgery and initially was not doing well. The nurse asked those of us in the community who could to come and do one hour shifts "kangaroo holding" the baby in hopes that the human touch and nurturing would help the baby to thrive. The family of the twins lives in a village very far away and they are unable to travel back and forth to the hospital. In the past two weeks, since starting the program, the baby has almost doubled her weight; she is off monitors and her feeding tube and getting very close to getting to go home.

My housemate Kate and I went today and spent time taking turns holding this precious baby girl. While we held her, we were able to speak life and hope over her little body. For the two hours we were there, she never closed her eyes or slept; she was very alert and was constantly looking at us. We were even allowed to feed her; she downed two large syringes of formula without hardly taking a breath.

As I sat and held this little baby and thanked God for her life, I couldn't help but notice the other babies in the room in incubators hooked up to IV's and feeding tubes. At the moment, there are three sets of triplets and four sets of twins in the NICU. Most of the families of these babies are ones who have traveled to India to have infertility treatment and are now back home hoping that at least one of their babies will live.

In this culture, the need to have a child is great, and that need pushes couples to the limit. I found myself struggling with conflicting emotions about the situation. Each one of the babies is a valuable gift from God, and yet the circumstances in which their lives exist are complicated. This hospital is the only one that is anywhere close to being able to support these tiny lives. They must turn families away every day because they do not have the room or the resources to take care of these high risk babies. It's difficult to understand, but there was a risk that this little baby I was holding today may have been abandoned had she not turned a corner. The family had one healthy baby to take home and cannot afford the cost of the other baby's hospitalization and certainly cannot take care of a "special needs" child who might need extra or long-term care. The staff was encouraged today as the father came by to see the baby, though he was already there because his mother-in-law was in the hospital.

With my Western thinking, it is hard to understand some of the situations and beliefs here. Sometimes there is a real lack of respect for life as people's hearts have been hardened due to the death that surrounds them every day. Most people do not celebrate birthdays and often can't tell you how old they are when you ask them. There is a great deal of superstition as well. Most believe that if you bring too much attention to adults, children, or babies, you will draw the attention of the evil spirits and the risk of something bad happening becomes greater. It's a very sad way to live; life is often fear-motivated instead of hope-motivated.

As I held this tiny baby girl today, I spoke life over her. I told her how much she was loved and treasured. I told her there was a plan and purpose for her, a plan that is good with a hope of greatness. I wondered what her "world" would be like as she enters adulthood, if her "world" would still be motivated by fear and hopelessness or if things would be different. I prayed that life would bring her advantages and education, knowledge that the world is bigger than Afghanistan and that she was created for good.

I hope to be able to go back several more times before she is released from the hospital. I hope to have a few more opportunities to speak life and hope over this beautiful child. I believe that God has opened a door for this little girl, a door for people to be able to speak truth over her, for people to pray for her health and provision. We cannot do everything for everyone, but if we take one day at a time and purpose to help one life at a time, change can happen!

As we enter this season when we celebrate hope, goodness, and truth, I am so grateful to have had the opportunity to hold this fragile little life and know that in her life is great potential for good. Holding that tiny baby reminded me of another baby who was born long ago and grew up to change the world; He later sacrificed His life so that we could find life.

Personal Reflections

Life and the circumstances surrounding it are most certainly complicated in Afghanistan. The simple joy of celebrating it most often doesn't exist. A new life here most often means another mouth to feed, another life to care for. For a mother who gives birth to a baby girl, she is saddened to know she will be seen as a burden to her family, someone who will be controlled by another, often abused, and used for others' gain. If a mother delivers a boy, she may have the approval of her husband and elders and mother-in-law; but she knows that this young boy will likely grow up to be a spoiled, overindulged youth who will then grow into a domineering and often angry, abusive, and addicted adult. There is often little for people to celebrate here. In our Western culture, we celebrate births and motherhood itself with great joy and fulfillment; we see our children as gifts and participate actively in their lives. I long for the mothers of Afghanistan to feel such emotion, to know that they are of great worth and their children priceless gifts from God. I know that life cannot exist without God and that He causes it to occur. Each time a child is born, God desires to show Himself as the Creator, as a loving and good God. Satan's agenda, however, is to keep people suppressed and in poverty and lack so that the knowledge of that truth never resonates.

When working with a local NGO, I was astonished to learn that women in the villages of Afghanistan feed their newborn babies butter that is made from cow or goat milk during their first week of life. Mothers believe colostrum, the yellowish liquid produced in the mother's breasts immediately following birth, is "weak" or "bad" milk and must not be given to the baby while waiting for the mother's real milk to come in. Simple education could teach these women that it has been scientifically proven that colostrum is full of antibodies and nutrition designed to give the baby the best possible start at life. Instead, the mothers are giving their babies something with little nutritional value and quite possibly endangering their delicate digestive systems.

The men also believe they have nothing to do with determining the sex of a baby. If a woman has girl after girl, most often the man will simply go out and find another wife in hopes of producing a male child. When my husband had the opportunity to teach the men that biologically the father determines the sex of a baby, they were astonished. Unfortunately, even education will not change some dangerous practices. Some beliefs are so ingrained into the culture that it will take generations to convince people to change their behavior.

Deuteronomy 30:19-20
I call heaven and earth as witnesses today against you, that I have set before you life and death, blessing and cursing; therefore choose life, that both you and your descendants may live; that you may love the Lord your God, that you may obey His voice, and that you may cling to Him, for He is your life and the length of your days.

CHAPTER 8 – Grace for the Day

James 4:6-8

But He gives more grace. Therefore He says: "God resists the proud, but gives grace to the humble." Therefore submit to God. Resist the devil and he will flee from you. Draw near to God and He will draw near to you.

Letter 28 - My Braveheart Man

As I sit down to write today, I realize that I haven't given you an update on what my husband is doing; so today is dedicated to my incredibly wonderful man!

Those of you who know my husband know that he is a combination of "The Man from Snowy River," "Braveheart," and "Indiana Jones." This adventure is right up his alley; he is in his element living each day doing exactly what he was made to do. Not to say this trip has not had its challenges, but the kind of challenges he encounters here are the ones that energize him instead of defeating him. He loves the opportunity to create something from nothing, finding all the ways a situation can succeed instead of fail. That is one of the things I love about him: he is an eternal optimist, always seeing the glass half full instead of half empty.

He jumped into the hospital work two weeks after we got here and hasn't slowed down once. In the three months since we arrived, the hospital inpatient volume has doubled. He has sponsored an OB emergency life support seminar that brought in doctors and midwives from all over the city. He has helped to get the surgery department up and running and even did overnight call in this hospital, setting the stage for true servant leadership.

Probably the highlight of these first few months for him was the opportunity he had to deliver a baby. Now I know that doesn't sound so out of the ordinary for him; at home he has delivered hundreds of them. It's a different story here, however, because of the culture; it is not acceptable for a male doctor to deliver a baby and was not something William thought he would have the privilege of doing while living here. While at work one day, a young woman was brought in while in labor. After several hours, the midwives came and told William that they would have to transport this woman to another hospital as the baby was in distress, and they couldn't get the baby

175

out. When William reviewed the case, it was clear that the woman, baby, or maybe both would not survive a transport. One midwife that trusts William very much knew that he probably had the skills to get the baby out, so she put up a sheet between the mother and William, put him in a gown and mask, and told him not to talk. The midwife brought William in and with hand signals, he was able to have the midwife tell the mother when to push and when not to. After several tense moments and removing the cord from around the baby's neck, William delivered a very large baby boy. Both mother and baby did very well. God had William at the right place at the right time. This incident has set the stage for more difficult OB cases to be taken care of in our hospital without a C-section and has created an opportunity for male doctors to learn from William how to care for high-risk maternity patients.

The one time I saw Will pretty frustrated was when a gentleman was brought to the hospital after being run over by a big truck. Our surgery center was not up and running yet, so William got in an ambulance with the gentleman in hopes of transporting him to the military trauma hospital. He spent an hour trying to resuscitate the gentleman while the ambulance sat in traffic, completely trapped and unable to move. By the time they reached the hospital, the gentleman had died. In this culture, you must bury a person the same day he dies; so the hospital would not take the patient, as the family was not there to claim his body. William had to ride around in traffic for another two hours with the dead gentleman until they found his family. He was so frustrated with the system here, knowing that if they had not gotten stuck in traffic, there might have been an opportunity to save this gentleman.

This past week, William had a friend bring in a young girl to see him; this young girl is pregnant and not married. In this culture, this is often grounds for being put to death; not for the father of the child, of course, but for the woman. It doesn't matter if the woman is a victim of rape or not; it is always seen as her fault, and she will pay the price.

He presented the patient to his colleagues and asked them what they should do. He said, "Let me remind you that as physicians, we have agreed to a set of values that is upheld by this hospital to treat any person in need of help, regardless of tribe or sex." The doctors were all upset as they said, "Yes, as doctors we should help; but our religion says we should put her to death." After a very good conversation, the doctors were willing to help this young woman. In the course of the conversation, one of the other doctors told a story of a time when a newborn baby was brought to him with most of its bones broken. The mother, who was 14 and unmarried and had been keeping her pregnancy a secret, was forced to dance at a wedding, after which she went into labor. After the baby was born, it was taken and beaten and thrown out, and the mother was set on fire with gasoline by her sister. This story set the stage for a very revealing dialogue about how to handle these situations in the future. Maybe at some point there can be some grace and respect offered to some unfortunate women as these young doctors set out on their own.

I wish you could all have the opportunity to meet these doctors with whom William works.. They all are amazingly bright and kind people. Each of these doctors has had challenge after challenge to be where they are. The commitment these men and women have made to medicine is astounding. William is having an incredible opportunity to invest into these doctors, teaching the kind of servant leadership skills as well as good medical skills that will take this country to a different level. It is a huge honor and privilege for William to be here working with these doctors.

Personal Reflections

Serving beside my husband for all these years has been an incredible ride. I have had the opportunity to travel to some of the most remote places in the world and have had the privilege of raising a half a dozen beautiful children with him. My husband is the complete opposite of most of the men in

Afghanistan and the perspective they have on women. He has always honored and respected me, celebrating my uniqueness. I may not have the medical skills that he has, and I don't put on a white coat each day for work, but he has always seen me as a partner in his life and calling. He works hard to include me in the details of what he does and affirms me in my jobs of support and caregiver to him and our children. When our family has moved to foreign soil so he can practice his gifts and skills in a hospital setting, it has been because our entire family was called and there were things that we each needed to do to fulfill the assignments given to us. When things are right for him, they are right for all of us.

Marriage can be difficult; and there are unique circumstances and challenges within a medical marriage. There are extreme time demands and a need for flexibility and fluid living as schedules and expectations have to constantly be adjusted. There is a risk in medical marriages for the doctor to receive a great deal of affirmation and encouragement for the "job well done," while the spouse is left in the background. There are demands that take the doctor away from family at the most inopportune times and lots and lots of situations that can lend to loneliness and feeling like the non-doctor spouse is carrying the brunt of the responsibility and load of the family and life.

My husband has made it his personal mission to let this happen as little as possible in our home. We are not perfect, and there have been some difficult years along the way with a schedule requiring 70-90 hours a week and a family of six kids and all that entails, but he has done an outstanding job balancing it all. When he comes home from the hospital, his white coat gets hung up, and he puts his daddy and husband hat on. He is completely immersed in his various roles in our family and miraculously finds time for it all. In spite of a demanding career, he has lived the example of a Godly father and husband, and I could not have more gratitude than

I do for that. My husband has never made me feel "less than" for choosing to stay home with our children and has always reminded me that I have great worth and relevance in my "world." He often says to me, "You have the harder job. Thank you for what you do."

I believe there were many times in the months we lived in Afghanistan that Will set a very high standard for the men around him. He showed the men of Afghanistan what it looks like to honor and treasure the gift of a wife. He spent long hours discussing what it means to honor and protect, not control and own. Though he never crossed cultural lines, he found ways to show the people around us that our marriage is one based on equality and respect; that the gifts that we have in each other are to be treasured and valued. He made it clear that we love each other and that we had to partner together to accomplish life's goals. I believe the way that he loves and lives with me is a testimony in itself, and I am honored to be part of that witness.

Ephesians 5:25-28

Husbands, love your wives, just as Christ also loved the church and gave Himself for her, that He might sanctify and cleanse her with the washing of water by the word, that He might present her to Himself a glorious church, not having spot or wrinkle or any such thing, but that she should be holy and without blemish. So husbands ought to love their own wives as their own bodies; he who loves his wife loves himself.

Letter 29 - A Tale of Two Cities

As I write, I'm sitting on a plane heading back home and feeling like an alien. The past forty-eight hours have put me somewhere near the moon.

We left Afghanistan just two days ago, heading home to spend the holidays with our older children and family. We decided that it would be wise to spend a few days in transition in Dubai. We had a wonderful time, but I don't know how much transition we went through; it actually felt like full-blown culture shock. Though Dubai and Kabul are only a two-hour plane ride apart from each other, they really couldn't be any farther apart than the earth and the moon.

Dubai is really like Disney World for adults. There are more malls per capita in Dubai than any other city in the world, and I'm not talking any old mall, but rather, malls that are more like works of art filled with any and every high end store that exists along with any kind of food you can imagine. On average, one mall could take you several hours just to go from one end to the other, especially if you spend time window shopping. Of course, window shopping is about the only thing the average tourist in Dubai can do unless you happen to be an oil sheik or have unlimited wealth. I honestly have never been in a place with as much excessive wealth as Dubai; even the wall clocks in the malls and at the airport are made by Rolex. If I don't want to window shop, I could snow ski indoors, go to the world's largest aquarium, ice skate, indoor skydive, or watch a different movie in every mall. Our family spent most of the time eating our way through the malls, indulging in all the things we have missed while living abroad: ice cream, fast food, chocolate, and of course, several trips a day to various coffee shops.

Dubai itself is an architectural wonder. It boasts the world's most modern and unusual structures. The tallest building in the world is attached to the Dubai mall and stands an impressive 160 floors tall. There is also a building under construction right now that will twist and turn itself in a complete circle every twenty-four hours. The skyline looks like the Emerald City; all the buildings are glass and reflect the sun as it sets and rises, making the city appear to glow and sparkle.

Along with the world's largest shopping malls and wonderfully impressive skyline is the beach; the Persian Gulf with its turquoise blue waters and powder fine sand is absolutely breathtaking. Perfect 80 degree weather made sitting on the beach and taking in the view one of the most memorable parts of the trip.

Now some of you may be thinking this place sounds perfect, and it was wonderful; but coming from where we have been living, it was really a bit much to take in at times. Every single aspect of our experience in Dubai was in complete contrast to everything we had become used to in Afghanistan. Central air and heat, regular electricity, instant hot water, the orderliness of things, the availability of things, the safety, and probably the best part...blending into the crowd and not being looked at like we have three heads.

We had a wonderful time together as a family and enjoyed all the incredible availability and variety of things; but, honestly, it was a bit confusing and left me wondering where to file all the sights and sounds and wonders we experienced.

Being in Dubai just reminded me that I live in between cultures right now; and though "home" is where my family is, even living there feels a bit foreign.

I know this break is good and much needed by us all. We are looking forward to our time with friends and family and all things familiar; but somehow we can't help but feel a bit like we are having an out of body experience, going through the motions of what we have lived with all our lives but at the same time feeling that it is all strangely unfamiliar and sometimes even feeling bad for what we have at our fingertips. I think we need as much grace returning as we needed going; it will take a few days for us to get our bearings, just in time to do it all over again!

Personal Reflections

Our visit home for Christmas was a much needed time of connecting with friends and family and though it brought little rest (quite the opposite), it did give us a renewed energy to push through and finish strong in what the Lord had in front of us.

We all spent the first few days in a trance, being in jetlag and overwhelmed with the chaos and activity of the holidays. My husband worked during the two weeks we were home, catching up on the happenings in the medical world; and the kids and I spent time with family and enjoying the season of Christmas!

The week before returning home from Afghanistan, my housemate Kate and I had a Christmas party for the female doctors at the hospital. All the ladies had been very inquisitive about the traditions of our American holiday. They wanted to know about Christmas trees and lights and ways that we celebrate as a family. Kate and I thought it would be fun to create a little "Christmas party" for the ladies and let them experience firsthand how we do things. We arrived at their break time and brought with us decorations and homemade candy and Christmas treats along with gifts for each of them. We spent a few hours just talking and answering questions about our traditions. The women were fascinated and so grateful for our time together. I felt it was a great opportunity to share with our friends the true meaning of the holiday; I can't talk about Christmas trees and lights and fudge and not talk about the baby born around Whom the entire holiday centers; or, should I say, I believe the Lord used the situation to present Himself to these beautiful women and give them an opportunity to feel loved and valued. Our little Christmas party was one of the highlights of our time in Afghanistan.

As I returned from our holiday, I spent time reflecting on

the contrast of my experiences. I was saddened to realize that in certain ways my Christmas in Afghanistan had more authentic relevance and meaning than my Christmas at home. Because of the absence of the Christmas holiday in a Muslim nation and because we lived with limited resources, we were forced to search for a meaningful expression of our favorite holiday. The result was an experience that challenged and authentically solidified my beliefs. We didn't need malls and lots of presents and parties and cards to worship Jesus. His gifts to us were abundant everywhere we looked—provision, friendships, family, and faith—all of which pointed us to the birth of our Savior. The freedoms of home didn't necessarily make our Christmas more authentic, rather they made it more complex, commercial and exhausting. I am grateful for the freedom of religion I enjoy at home, but I am also very grateful that I was allowed to experience a Christian holiday in a Muslim country. It was one of my greatest gifts of the year.

Luke 2:10-11
Then the angel said to them, "Do not be afraid, for behold, I bring you good tidings of great joy which will be to all people. For there is born to you this day in the city of David a Savior, who is Christ the Lord."

Letter 30 - A Blanket of Grace

Today marks a week since our return to Afghanistan. I swear it seems we have actually been back a month; time is so weird living in a developing country. Sometimes time seems to stand still, creeping by minute by minute, feeling that I am standing still while everyone and everything is passing me by at a hundred miles an hour. Other times, it seems like a week has gone by, and it's actually been a month. A week of experiences is actually the equivalent to months anywhere else. Every time I travel in this city, even just to the store, I feel exhausted when I return because there has been so much visual and auditory stimulus during my time out that I can hardly process it all. I can travel the same route ten times in a week and never see the same things twice. The buzz of life is astounding, and that buzz is so unorganized and chaotic that I can never really feel relaxed. Traffic is going four different directions, people coming and going, buying and selling, arguing and laughing, horns blaring and sirens screeching, fires burning, shepherds herding livestock, mullahs calling to prayer, and policemen blowing whistles, all happening at the same time. When I combine this stimulus with jetlag and culture adjustment, I swear I can think that I'm on another planet, not just in another country.

It's been a month since I have written, and in that time we have traveled to Dubai and then to home, visited with family and friends, celebrated two holidays and three birthdays, shopped and repacked and organized our lives and family to live in two countries for the months to come. During this time I have felt a million different emotions, experiencing extreme reverse culture shock and a deep sense of gratitude for this crazy life I get to live. I was completely shocked at how hard it was to be back in America; though it's my country of origin and my cultural home, things seemed very foreign to me; the pace, the variety, and the availability of things seemed so strange and unfamiliar. Don't get me wrong, my hot showers, comfy bed, and trips to Sonic were the best; but everything coming all at once was a bit too much at times. I battled extreme feelings of inadequacy. I felt like I couldn't quite live up to the standards around me, not projected from those I love, but by society itself. I had a hard time reconciling everything from the two worlds and the extremes in which I find myself living.

I am happy to be back in my little "hobbit" house living a slower, quieter, simpler life. Life in the last week has most certainly been simple. We have been without electricity almost half of the time; no electricity means no hot water, no internet, no music, no movies, no lights, no hairdryer, no washer, no Skyping, no toaster, no vacuum, no printer, etc. You get the picture, just the basics. Fortunately, our heaters burn either wood or kerosene, so staying warm has not been a problem. Days are short when I have only the sunlight or candles to see by. Suddenly, 8:00 p.m. really feels like midnight.

My host country has been through some changes this week as well. The day after we returned, a suicide bomber blew himself up next to a bus filled with Afghan security personnel, killing four and wounding twenty-plus. The explosion happened just two miles from our home; all our windows shook with the blast. The children's school went on lock down, keeping everyone safe inside. I could hear sirens for hours. We were not scared, just saddened for the people of this country and acutely aware of how fragile things are. The civil war that is flamed by human pride and anger here is destroying a generation—not only lives, but growth and expansion as well. This country has known nothing but violence and destruction for thirty straight years. The sadness that is worn like a blanket on the people of Afghanistan is taking its toll. You can see the hopelessness in people's eyes; children who don't laugh and play because their little minds are consumed with staying warm and fed and safe. Living here, I have to battle each day to keep hope in my heart for a better day for these people. There is a God who loves them so much, whose heart is breaking for the suffering going on here. I have to remember that God wants to use His people to ease that suffering and restore a sense of hope; that's what gets me up each day and keeps me from weeping for hours for the despair and lack of hope around me.

This week we have learned that Iran is putting a ban on fuel being imported into Afghanistan. It's a long and complicated story; but this ban will double fuel prices here, making it twice as hard for people to work, stay warm, and live. Most of the food and supplies used here in the city are imported from neighboring countries. With fuel doubling in price, the goods that are brought in will also double in cost. The difficult life for Afghans just got considerably worse. The fuel changes will be quite difficult for the foreign community as well, pushing the already high cost of living here through the roof.

On top of the news from Iran and the bombing, January has been the driest and warmest one for years. Usually the winter, though cold and hard on the people, is still tolerable because it brings snow. There is an Afghan saying that states that the snow on the mountains is more valuable than all the gold in the world, meaning that without the snow, this country suffers greatly. Snow means water, and water is the lifeline for all that grows and flourishes here. Though the mild temperatures have been a nice reprieve for the people, everyone is heavy-hearted wondering if there will be enough water in the spring. There are only six weeks of winter left; all are praying that February will be white.

It has been said that we receive grace each day, new every morning... that is my prayer for this nation, that a blanket of fresh grace will fall here each and every day; a grace to live, not just to survive, but to actually thrive.

Personal Reflections

The traditional men of this country do not wear coats in the winter; they wear a large wool cape called a patu that they wrap around themselves like a blanket. As I pray for the people of Afghanistan, I have a visual image of God's grace and love being dropped down and wrapped around these people like a patu of love. There are so many things wrong with this country, so much need and lack, that looking at things in the natural will just bring hopelessness, fear, and heaviness.

Without God we can do nothing, so I have to rely on His power and ability to change lives, one at a time. I can make myself available, but it's He who has to do the work. Even in prayer, it's my responsibility to remind God of the needs of the people and to stand in the gap for them, asking Him to do the work, to send His grace, provision, and help. Then I have to leave it with Him and let Him see it through.

Fear is a dominating, strong emotion permeating this land. Fear occupies every moment of every day for these people. At times it seems almost visible, like smoke winding in and out of every crevice and lurking in every corner. Fear affects the choices and decisions of all Afghans; it directs conversations and actions. It lurks behind every wall of every home sucking the joy, peace, and breath from the Afghans who live there. The Bible tells us fear can be paralyzing. A person who is paralyzed is not dead; he or she simply cannot move or speak. That is what fear has done to the Afghans; it has paralyzed them from moving forward, from doing anything but merely existing. Fear is what keeps the nation of Afghanistan from advancing; it keeps people from knowing truth and peace. Because of the dark presence of fear paralyzing and dominating the people, there is no foundation of trust between individuals.

Lack of trust is one of the biggest problems the international troops have working in Afghanistan. How can Afghans trust a foreigner when they can't even trust their own family member? Afghanistan is in civil war, tribe against tribe, every man for himself and his family. There is very little cooperation and partnership in the Afghan culture. The need for survival breeds mistrust and secrecy. It is impossible to expect a democracy to function in a society that knows only tribal warfare and the realities of a dictatorship. The international forces should not expect the leaders of Afghanistan to react to challenges and situations like others would; they don't know how. And though freedom and equality is the cry of every heart in Afghanistan, because of thirty years of continuous war and conflict, it has never been experienced or modeled for most of them. They are in some ways like children learning how to play together in a sand box. They need to learn that cooperating and working together and sharing resources and valuing each other leads to peace and success for all.

John 1:14-17

And the Word became flesh and dwelt among us, and we beheld His glory, the glory as of the only begotten of the Father, full of grace and truth. John bore witness of Him and cried out, saying, "This was He of whom I said, 'He who comes after me is preferred before me, for He was before me.' " And of His fullness we have all received, and grace for grace. For the law was given through Moses, but grace and truth came through Jesus Christ.

CHAPTER 9 – The Fragile Thread of Freedom

Galatians 5:1

Stand fast therefore in the liberty by which Christ has made us free, and do not be entangled again with a yoke of bondage.

Letter 31 - Behind the Veil

The police have visited our neighborhood quite regularly the past several weeks, interviewing our guards and drivers and neighbors. It seems that there has been a prostitution business being run in the house right next door to us. The house is less than five feet from ours. I can almost reach across the span from my terrace to the window of the house. I have often stood on my terrace and watched young children at play in the front yard, listening to the sounds of life.

How can I live so close to a situation, even hearing and smelling the life going on, and never know of the injustices taking place behind a wall I can almost touch?

My heart is grieved for women and children caught up in this horrible situation; they are the true victims here. What kind of woman, especially in this culture, could get caught up in this lifestyle? A woman who is desperate to survive; a woman who will go to great lengths, even risking her life, to provide for her family; a woman who is owned and controlled by evil in the form of an angry, deceived man.

Some of you may argue that working in the profession of prostitution is a woman's choice, but I would beg to differ with you in this place. Prostitution is punishable by death in this culture; not for the man, of course, only for the woman. It is understood that whatever actions of inappropriateness are committed by a man are solely the fault of the woman, as she must have enticed or forced him. Most prostitutes in this country are well hidden and not cared for. Most are exposed to and forced to smoke opium which is very addictive and gives the "owners" control over their workers. Like drugs and weapons in this country, women bring a huge profit.

I have thought of these young women and children so often the past few days, wondering what has become of them, hoping they are still alive. The house is empty except for a "For Rent" sign on the front wall. There are no sounds of laughter and life, only empty rooms and walls; and, if they could speak, they would tell story after story of abuse and pain. Soon people will begin to visit the house, considering it for their home, never knowing what tragedy has gone on there.

This incident has led me to consider the lives and hidden pains of others around me. In this country with all the cultural taboos and burka-clad women, it's easy to distance myself from the truth that every woman and child represents a life, a family, joys, sadness, hopes, fears and pains. We have heard the stories of abuse by husbands and injustices done to women here. The hard thing is that those stories are attached to "real" people in this "real" place. It's really no different in my home country. Though we are free to uncover our arms and heads and faces, we still go through our lives on a daily basis seeing and being in contact with people who conceal the pain and suffering of abuse and heartache. Maybe the abuse is not as life threatening and powerful as prostitution; but everyone carries wounds and scars of hate, rejection and fear. It's easy to go about our lives so consumed with what is right in front of us that we are unable to recognize the signs of pain and injustice.

I can't help but wonder whether, had I paid closer attention, I would have seen some signs. Maybe in some way I could have been a part of restoration and help instead of selfishness and indifference. I don't know the language and culturally it would not have been appropriate to visit, but I could have made myself available for a smile or encouragement, and I could have prayed. I could have lifted the situation up to a Father who cares and grieves at the pain and injustice in this world. I could have stood in their behalf, crying with a voice that they do not have.

In this place especially, it becomes very easy to be overwhelmed with the need and pain of this forgotten land. I must not become so

191

calloused and self-centered that I do not look for individual situations and people to support, love, and care for. God sees these people. He sees individuals with a purpose and beauty all their own, and so should I.

I challenge you, and myself, to look for an opportunity to share hope and love with someone: Maybe a rude cashier or the person standing behind you in a line; maybe the mail person who has been delivering your mail for years, but you have never taken the time to know his name; maybe it's a total stranger you pass on a morning walk or park next to in a parking lot. Begin to see the masses as individuals with the same hopes and dreams and hurts and failures as you have. Maybe an act or word can make all the difference in a person's life or situation. Yes, maybe it will be awkward or embarrassing; but what can be the worst thing to happen - that you will be seen as caring? Take that chance!

Personal Reflection

We have no idea what is behind the veils of the lives of people. It's so easy to judge people by their actions when we have no idea what motivates them. I can't imagine navigating through life with some of the burdens and pain that others have, certainly doing so without the Lord. A well known preacher made a statement years ago that made such an impact on me that I am reminded of it almost daily. She said, "Hurting people hurt people." Wow! So simple and so true. If we can see that there are hurts and disappointments and tragedy every day in the lives of people which motivate them and enable them to project those feelings onto others, maybe we could try to be more patient and understanding. Be determined to extend grace and forgiveness on a daily basis; it will bring a new level of freedom to your own life. At the same time, look for these situations as opportunities to ask the Holy Spirit to work in the lives of people. Stand in the gap for those who doesn't know how to do that for themselves. Ask God to do a work in people's lives. Notice them, care about them, help them, and allow God's love to show through you. Ask God to show you life through His eyes. Ask Him to let you see people the way He does. If you dare allow that kind of revelation into your heart, you will be astonished at what you will find. You will learn to live life from a new perspective, God's perspective; and with that will come a new level of compassion, sensitivity, purpose and joy.

Ephesians 1:7-10

In Him we have redemption through His blood, the forgiveness of sins, according to the riches of His grace which He made to abound toward us in all wisdom and prudence, having made known to us the mystery of His will, according to His good pleasure which He purposed in Himself, that in the dispensation of the fullness of the times He might gather together in one all things in Christ, both which are in heaven and which are on earth—in Him.

Letter 32 - Holding Our Breath

We had another bombing yesterday, this time a local grocery store that is frequented by foreigners. At first the Taliban was taking credit for the blast, but now it looks like they may have had nothing to do with it. The speculation now is that an Iranian insurgent group may be responsible.

Today I'm heavy with emotion. I'm not sure where to put everything I feel. This particular bomb, unlike the others, is not in my periphery; its right smack in front of me. The place this bomb exploded is a place I visit weekly. This particular store is one that much of the expat community enjoys. The Western style store stocks all of our favorite items and gives us all an opportunity to feel a sense of "home" when we shop there. It's very common to run into several people I know while shopping.

There are two branches of this particular store, one in midtown and one out by our house. On this particular day, my husband and I were actually shopping at the branch store by our home when the blast occurred. We got a phone call from our office manager that something in the community had happened, and we should head home. As I look back now, I can remember that all the personnel in the store were strangely quiet and awkward. Usually the clerks will chat with me and be very friendly. This particular day, the store was very quiet; no one talking and no one interacting. As I thought about it, I am sure they all knew what had just happened. They were trying to stay calm for us, but I am sure they were all scared and worried, not only for themselves, but for their friends and fellow co-workers.

When we arrived at home, we found out that the blast had occurred at the midtown store. Within minutes, we were able to pull up information and pictures on the internet. It was a very strange feeling to be so familiar with the images I was seeing. As the video footage scanned the store, I could tell you where everything used to be. I could tell you the exact spot in the store the victims would have been standing and where the suicide bomber must have detonated his bomb. As I looked at the pictures of items blown out into the street, I could have told you where the milk should have gone and where the eggs should be.

Today we know that four foreigners were killed in the blast and it's assumed that some were Americans, but we still don't know their names or whether they were people we know personally. I suppose that shouldn't matter; loss of life is a tragedy whether we know a person personally or not. It's still hard, though, to wait for the names to be released.

We did find out this morning that one of our staff members had two family members affected by the blast. Both worked for the grocery store; one was killed and one badly injured. I can't help wonder if I would recognize their faces if I saw them. The young men who worked in the store were always so helpful and kind.

The expat community is holding its breath right now, waiting to see what happens. Some of our friends are concerned that their agencies will send them back to their home countries. People in the expat community have invested a lot into this country; it would be a tragedy for them to have to leave it all behind.

I realized, as this was unfolding, that the Afghans with whom we are in relationship all take huge risks to partner with us. There are many enemies of foreigners that lurk not only here in our borders but elsewhere as well. When an Afghan agrees to work for or be in relationship with us, they are doing so at risk to themselves and/or their families. I don't know if any of the young Afghans who lost their lives yesterday had ever considered that risk, or just saw their positions as a way to make a living. It's weird to think of myself in a position to put others in harm's way, especially when I feel I am here to help and support the hurting people of this country. In reality though, I do put them at risk every day. These men drive us, cook for us, protect us, and serve us, all knowing that they do so with a price.

Our chowkidar (guard) told us last week that he can't go home very often anymore and when he does, he must stay in his house because the Taliban know foreigners employ him, and therefore he is not safe.

This revelation is another opportunity to again be grateful for my home country. When is the last time you knew of someone who worried for their safety every time they left for work? I am very grateful that my family and friends have a safe environment in which to provide for themselves and their families.

The sadness and heaviness I feel today is like a huge wool blanket suffocating me. The sadness I feel is not for myself, but for this nation.

The evil here is stripping this country of people and things that can bring hope and change. Evil is like that, isn't it? So selfish, so one-sided, the only thing it cares about is itself; it doesn't care who is in its way or who is affected in the wake of its destruction; it only cares for its own agenda.

These attacks in this country are against government, against foreigners, against Afghans, against religion; but it really doesn't matter. The target, the outcome, is always the same: destruction, loss, and pain. The destruction and pain don't only affect the targets; they also affect this nation itself and the hearts of its precious people. The people of this country are so deceived and confused that they don't know where the truth lies; they don't know who to believe.

I am grateful that in these uncertain dark days, I know where truth is. I do know that no matter how bad things get, there is always hope. The light cannot ever be completely snuffed out; there is always a remnant left. The "Light" will always make sure that there are those who will stand in the gap for this place; and though there may come a time when we cannot physically be here, we will always be connected in spirit and prayer. Afghanistan, you are not forgotten!

Personal Reflection

After returning to America, I have had to remind myself of the remnant of "Light" in Afghanistan. Things continue to worsen by the day. I sense that there may come a day soon that it will be very difficult for people of the Truth to stay there. Even now, it's hard to continue their work and stay focused on what they are doing, as there are so many difficulties with security and safety. Remembering that God will continue to bring light into this dark place, even if His people are forced out, is comforting to me. Afghanistan will not be forgotten by Him or those of us whose hearts have been imprinted with this nation and its people.

I often think of the Afghans who have risked and continue to risk their lives for the foreign community. I am humbled by their sacrifices. At the same time, I know that the provisions of the Lord and the protection of His hand will be extended toward them for helping God's plans and purposes be fulfilled there, even without their knowledge. God will bless these people for being a blessing; that is how the laws of His world work. I love that! I also believe that if a time comes when God's helpers are removed from this country, the people who have helped and supported the efforts there will reflect on situations and conversations and will see the Truth in them! God accomplishes things differently than we do; He sees and knows the hearts of men and He will be the one to judge them, not us!

2 Chronicles 7:14

If My people who are called by My name will humble themselves, and pray and seek My face, and turn from their wicked ways, then I will hear from heaven, and will forgive their sin and heal their land.

Letter 33 - The Gift of Freedom

It's been a little over a week since the bombing at the local grocery, and we are all settled into a new kind of "normal." It's hard to believe it's only been a week. Time is so weird here; it seems like it has been at least a month since the deadly explosion. Maybe that is because of all that is going on in Egypt and other parts of the world; it seems like there is no way it all could have happened just a week ago.

There has been a lot of speculating about who was actually responsible for the bombing. Several groups have stepped forward and claimed responsibility, but few who have investigated this tragedy believe any of them had anything to do with it all. The latest information is leaning toward the theory that a hired mercenary group from Iran is responsible. The group was hired to target a prominent Afghan family living here in Kabul, a young surgeon and his wife and their four children, all who were killed in the blast. The young woman, a lawyer, was scheduled to meet with the New York Times *that very afternoon to share a story of child sex trafficking and human rights violations going on in this country.*

The layers are many with a story like this one. Though many are aware of the injustices done here, very few are brave enough to speak out against them. The shaming and defaming that would go along with the knowledge of the truth is more than most can bear. Still others are threatened by the potential loss of income and business that a story like this one would bring.

Freedom of speech is not a reality in this place. This situation has brought that to the forefront. Though most know that true freedom of speech is not a reality here, some still hold on to the hope that it isn't as bad as they thought. This situation has the national community in as much distress as the foreign community. The risks of standing up for change are high and have caused many people to reevaluate life in this place.

We in the foreign community have come to grips with the fact that there will now be a new "normal" for us. Though we have always been restricted somewhat in when and where we move about this city, things have gotten significantly tighter. Many of the restaurants and shops that we are used to going to are now off limits; and unless there is a necessary reason to travel, we have been asked to stay home.

Though I am tempted, at times, to feel sorry for myself at my loss of "freedom," it is nothing compared to what the people of Afghanistan deal with every day, their loss of freedom or, maybe I should just say, lack of freedom. Most people are able to go about their day conducting business and trying to care for their families, but they all do it at great risk to themselves and their families. They do not have the freedom to speak their minds, to stand up for wrongs and injustices done to them or to others they know. Bribing, cheating, stealing, and lying are all common ways to conduct business, even by the police. Many children still do not have the opportunity of free and appropriate education. They often spend their days hauling water and cutting wood for their families. The women do not have freedom to choose who they marry or where they work or if they want to drive or travel or even who to speak to. The people are ruled by heavy taskmasters standing behind the mask of religion, and those heavy-handed tyrants are using religion to control them.

This lack of freedom and the injustices are precisely what our forefathers in America fought so hard for: the right to choose, the right to speak, the right to believe, and the right to learn. Often we take these gifts for granted. We forget, on a daily basis, that men and women gave their lives to give us the freedoms we have, the freedoms that we know as "individual rights." These freedoms are not "entitlements;" they are gifts that all people should have the "right" to enjoy. We experience these freedoms because someone else was willing to pay the price for them.

So the question I have now, after living in this forgotten land, is, "Who will fight for these people? Who will stand up against the injustices of this nation?" Do we not have a moral obligation to help those in need, to stand up for those who cannot stand up for themselves? I know these are hard questions and at times, ones without answers. I'm not sure how much I am willing to risk for change, but I do know that God loves these people and His heart aches with the injustices done to them. But doesn't God need voices and bodies to transfer His love? There must be those who are willing to fight a battle because others cannot fight for themselves. There have to be those willing to give and do because it was given and done for them. And there must be those who are willing to risk just because it's right!

Now that I cannot go out as much, I spend a lot of time standing on my terrace looking over this crippled city. The view, sometimes breathtaking with the snowcapped mountains in the background, is often humbling as I remember what an honor it is to live in this place among these forgotten people.

"God, give me the grace and ability to live beyond myself, to live a life of conviction and faith for those things that are dear to Your heart!"

Personal Reflection

The things I was wrestling with in this letter are things that I continue to wrestle with on a daily basis. Seeing life through the lens of God's perspective, loving and serving with His motivation, and being willing to live a life bigger than my insecurities and myself is not easy. Living in Afghanistan was a beautiful and humbling gift. It was an honor to walk side-by-side with another culture, with all of its beauty and tragedy. I felt the same kind of honor living there that I had when witnessing the birth of a friend's baby or being in the presence of a close friend as he lived out his final moments in this world. Life is precious and sacred, and the moments we are given are gifts, no matter how joyful or hard.

Now that I am physically separated from Afghanistan it has become harder to hold on to the treasures I received there. Life sucks and pulls at the lessons I learned and the revelations I received and attempts to replace them with trivial, meaningless details. I am learning new lessons of finding roses in my own culture and life now. At times it is harder living here than it was there. Life is comfortable and manageable, but too self-centered. In some ways the prayer that I prayed in Afghanistan seems more difficult while I am living here, though the heart of the matter is the same. No matter what my life looks like—stepping over opium addicts in the streets and navigating security checkpoints, or sitting on the sidelines cheering on my children in their athletic events—my prayer is the same. "God, give me the grace and ability to live beyond myself, to live a life of conviction and faith for those things that are dear to Your heart!"

2 Corinthians 3:17-18
Now the Lord is the Spirit; and where the Spirit of the Lord is, there is liberty. But we all, with unveiled face, beholding as in a mirror the glory of the Lord, are being transformed into the same image from glory to glory, just as by the Spirit of the Lord.

Letter 34 - Our Trip to Chiang Mai

When we made the decision to move to Afghanistan, we also made a commitment to attend a conference in Thailand. When we made the decision to go, we knew it would be a great opportunity for us and our children to experience yet another culture. We did not know, however, how timely this trip would be. A break from our current situation and culture was greatly needed and very much appreciated. In the past month, we have had three bombings which have restricted our movement and freedom a great deal. We have also had almost constant rain and snow; I think I counted three days in the last month with sun. Though the country is in great need of moisture, and we are all relieved that the rain has come, the dreariness has made keeping an upbeat outlook on life rather difficult. Combine constant rain, intermittent electricity, frigid temperatures, and restriction to a 700 square foot apartment... a setup for depression for sure.

Our journey to Thailand began a day earlier than expected, when a huge snowstorm came through Kabul. We knew the snow would create delays and even possible cancelations in flights, so we decided to try to get to Dubai a day early. We picked the kids up early from school on Saturday and headed to the airport. On the way, our driver got into an accident and almost ended up in a fistfight. The police came and broke it up, and what could have been hours of delay ended up being only a few minutes. After arriving at the airport, check-in and immigration went smoothly; we even boarded relatively close to the original departure time. After boarding the plane though, things didn't go so smoothly. We sat on the plane for three hours while the airport used the only snowplow in Kabul to clear the runway, and after de-icing the plane, we finally got off the ground. At least we have a snow plow and the ability to de-ice; otherwise we may have never made it out. We found out the flight we were scheduled on for the next day was cancelled.

We arrived in Dubai about midnight, thrilled to be in warm weather and at the airport where our Bangkok connection would depart from. We spent the next day in Dubai walking the crazy malls and even went to a movie. While walking through the mall, I saw an Emirate family walking with their baby who was in a stroller watching Barney on a portable DVD player attached to the front of the stroller. The DVD player was actually part of the stroller construction! That pretty much sums up Dubai for you.

We took the midnight flight to Bangkok and arrived around 8:00 a.m. From the airport, we took a taxi to the train station, stored our luggage, and set out to see the city. We spent the day riding tuk tuks (motorcycles with a canopy car attached) around the city visiting temples, silk stores, and shopping centers. That evening we boarded the night train heading to Chiang Mai. The kids have never been on a train before, so we thought taking the more scenic route to the mountains would be the way to go. Our family shared a sleeping car with four bunks, two on the bottom and two on top, complete with our own personal entertainment (our train stewardess who was really a steward who was really trying hard to impress my husband). The train would have been perfect for a good night's sleep except that it made a dozen stops in fourteen hours. By the time we reached Chiang

Mai, I had gone two days and nights without much more than a few hours of sleep.

After arriving in Chiang Mai, we hired a taxi to take us the one hour drive into the mountains to our conference center. As we drove, I fell more and more in love with Thailand. The beautiful green mountains with wild orchids growing up the trees, banana trees, palm trees, and rice patties were breathtaking. I had not realized how starved for green I was. In Kabul, everything is gray and dirty and harsh looking. Here, the landscape is painted with color and life, about as opposite a place as one could imagine.

Today after a breakfast with fresh fruit and fresh squeezed orange juice and a lunch with green salad and vegetables, we headed out for a walk. As I took everything in—the green grass, the purple, pink, and red bougainvillea, the palm trees and wild orchids—I was almost brought to tears. The realization that I could walk in public with shorts and a sleeveless shirt and not be offensive (except for blinding all I met with my white skin) was a crazy feeling. I even enjoyed the fact that it was 90 degrees, and I was sweating! Stopping to think that I could move about ALONE was almost more than I could shoulder. What a gift this place is. God always knows exactly what we need even before we do. He knew last summer that Thailand would be just the perfect gift for us all.

God even knew what our kids would need. This particular conference brought families from all over the world, but especially from Southeast Asia and mainly Western families that live in host countries. The conference has a special kids' program designed just for them. Each day they go to breakfast and we don't see them again until dinner as they are doing activities and games with trained leaders who have come to Thailand just for them. The kids made special friends the first day; these friends understand what it is like to live abroad and the challenges of leaving their friends and home countries. I think for the first time in six months, the kids felt like they belonged and were a part of a group of kids like themselves. God is so good!

So for the next week, after my husband finishes attending classes and lectures, we will get to do some special things. We will ride elephants, do a zip line through the jungle, go to a Thai cultural dinner and show, river raft, go to an orchid and butterfly farm, pet tigers, and go to a Thai cooking class. I can't think of anything more wonderful right now, except maybe getting to do all of this with our other children and family. This trip is like a big bear hug from God!

Personal Reflection

There are a lot of fringe benefits to being obedient to the Lord. One of our favorite things to do is travel. We love to visit new cultures and experience new places. We love to see and appreciate the beautiful diversity of this world and God's creative hand. Getting to visit Thailand during our time in Afghanistan was most certainly one of those fringe benefits of obedience. Just like we love to give wonderful surprises and gifts to our children as they grow, God loves to do that for His children. He loves to give us what we love and what speaks the most love to us. In our case, it was the treat of getting to experience places in the world we normally would not be able to visit. For our children, getting to experience all of this with new friends and peers who understand them was truly a blessing. The gift of this trip is something they will take with them throughout their lives.

God knows us better than we know ourselves. He plans and orchestrates things to speak love to us each and every day. We get so busy that we often miss them. Take time to see the little and big things in your life in which God speaks love to you. Let Him wrap His arms around you as He places things in your life that speak love to you personally. God is a good Father, and He wants to give to His children!

Luke 11:9-13

So I say to you, ask, and it will be given to you; seek, and you will find; knock, and it will be opened to you. For everyone who asks receives, and he who seeks finds, and to him who knocks it will be opened. If a son asks for bread from any father among you, will he give him a stone? Or if he asks for a fish, will he give him a serpent instead of a fish? Or if he asks for an egg, will he offer him a scorpion? If you then, being evil, know how to give good gifts to your children, how much more will your heavenly Father give the Holy Spirit to those who ask Him!

Letter 35 - We're Back

We have been out of the loop a bit but are now back in K-town settling in for the last push before heading home.

Thailand was an amazing gift. I had no idea how refreshing it would be to be in a country where we could wear what we wanted and go where we wanted, to walk down the street and have no one stare at me, to soak up the warm sun by being outside, and to eat some of the most amazing fruits in the world. It was just what we all needed!

I have to be honest and say, though, that experiencing all the blessings of Thailand made it hard to think about coming back to our little "hobbit house" and the cold, restricted life here. The feelings took me by surprise, as I didn't experience them at all after our trip home to America in December. When the time came, I was ready to return and was excited to get back to work. This time though, I dreaded it and even got anxious thinking about it. Though I have never felt afraid to live here, I think the security issues and restrictions affect us more than we think. There was another bombing while we were gone, again at a place we frequent often, and more talk of security restrictions.

The lack of beauty here really gets to us after a while as well. On a walk while we were in Thailand, I couldn't help but note how strikingly different things there were. It was green and beautifully lush, wild flowers growing everywhere. I was wearing Capris and a short-sleeved shirt, people passing us never even glancing our way, yards trimmed and neat. In contrast, while on a rare walk in Kabul just a few days before leaving on our trip, I was wearing an abaya and chadar, every inch of my body covered. We walked a path around a school and had to step over human waste as the rains had forced the open sewers to flood the path. At one point, as I stepped over the open jewie, I had to step over a floating dead dog. We passed opium addicts asleep on the ground. Only dirt and trash as far as we could see, no grass, no trees, no manicured lawns; only high walls and security, barbed wire, and guards, and guns. No blending in either; every single person we passed had to look long and hard at every inch of me.

I feel badly drawing these contrasts; it's not really fair. One country is free and one bound by war and deception. For the most part, it's not the fault of these people in Afghanistan that things are as bad as they are. It's like blaming and disliking a child who is difficult to tolerate as he throws a temper tantrum and misbehaves when, really, the behavior might be the parent's fault. Whoever's fault it is, it's still difficult to stomach at times.

On a much happier note, Said Musa was released from prison this week and taken safely out of the country. If you don't know, Said is an Afghan man who has been imprisoned and abused and tortured for the past nine months for changing his religion from Islam to Christianity. The Afghan constitution states that this is not against the law, but the arrest still happened. Many, many people from around the world have been working for Said's release; and this month, after pressure from several countries, what seemed impossible happened! Many in the foreign and Afghan community here rejoice in this injustice turned around and pray that it will open the doors for others in the same situation. *This is a victory in the fight against injustice and will be an example and encouragement to many around the world.*

As I write this, we are entering the last phase of our time here in Afghanistan. In ten short weeks we will be back home. I have very mixed feelings about this fact. As hard as things have been here, my heart is heavy at the thought of leaving. I feel, in a way, that I will be abandoning the people here, both foreign and national. There is so much to still be done, so far to go. I know that no matter how good my intentions are and how hard I work, the problems of this country are too big for me to shoulder. We knew when we started that this would be a short-term situation and that there would not be time to do all that we wanted. When I am faced with that reality though, it's much harder to reconcile than I thought it would be. There are men and women who have given their lives to the advancement of things here; who was I to think I could make a dent in such a short time?

On the other side of that coin, I know that we are doing what we are supposed to be doing in the only time frame possible. I have to trust God for all the rest.

I know, as the time gets shorter, I will wrestle with and write about this process more; so you will have to bear with me. For now though, I will look at today and what can be done and trust God for tomorrow!

Personal Reflection

The day in which we are living is really all that any of us have. No one has been promised or assured of more than what is in front of them. No matter how hard we look to the future and fret about what might come, there is nothing we can do about it. My mother-in-law always told my children as they were growing up, "Enjoy the moment; don't worry about later; just enjoy right now." It's so true. Sometimes we get so caught up in what we will be doing or even what we have already done that we lose the gift of the moment we are living. The moment we are living in is what the Lord has given us to be most effective and relevant for what is in the future. Without being all that we can be right now, how can we be what we need to be in the situations to come? How many times do we miss the blessings of today because of the fear or anticipation of tomorrow? We need to learn to live in the "right now" whether it's good or bad; the present moment has things to teach us and give to us. Take time today to just "enjoy the moment," love where you are, and allow God to be all He is right now in your situation.

Hebrews 13:5
Keep your lives free from the love of money and be content with what you have, because God has said, "Never will I leave you; never will I forsake you." (New International Version)

CHAPTER 10 – Hidden Pain

Isaiah 53:5

But He was wounded for our transgressions, He was bruised for our iniquities; the chastisement for our peace was upon Him, and by His stripes we are healed.

Letter 36 - Difficult Choices

Last night I laid in the dark listening to my husband talk on the phone to one of his colleagues at the hospital. He was trying to talk the doctor though delivering a dead baby that was stuck inside the mother. As I listened to him explain what to do, I was once again overwhelmed with sadness for this country. There is not a week that goes by at the hospital that they don't deliver a baby that has died. There are a lot of reasons why this happens so often here, but the bottom line is that it's a horrible tragedy that in most cases shouldn't happen.

Afghanistan has one of the highest infant and maternal morbidity rates of any country. Most women still deliver in the villages with a midwife, as they are forbidden to be examined by a male doctor. With the education of women so limited, there is not much hope for improving those statistics right now.

As I listened to the conversation my husband was having, I couldn't help but think about my own six deliveries as well as the three babies I lost by miscarriage. All the medical care I received in those situations was state of the art; I never once felt that all the doctors and nurses were not doing all they could to assure I not only had a good outcome, but also a positive experience. I never wondered or worried about the lack of skill or supplies if anything should go wrong. I never worried about how I was going to get up that day and cook for my family or take care of my other children. I was always given ample time to recover and was even supported through the process. I delivered all my children in a hospital with clean instruments and sheets, medicine, and food. I was allowed to stay and received visitors who celebrated with me and even brought me gifts of congratulations. I went home a few days later where I had family and friends cooking and cleaning for me, taking on my duties so I could recover and enjoy my new baby.

In stark contrast, I thought of the women here giving birth at home, praying and hoping that nothing goes wrong. No medication, no clean instruments, no blood bank or back up surgery unit, no incubators or oxygen, no warm showers or Jacuzzi tub. There are no warming beds for the babies or real medical support if the baby is sick or not breathing correctly. There are no sutures or pain medicines for the mother. If nothing goes wrong, these women are expected to get up the same day and take care of their families.

In a rural clinic we visited, women come in to deliver their babies so they can have a doctor present. They labor on a metal table in a room with only a wood burning stove for heat, no running water, and no recovery room. If the delivery has been "normal," the mom walks back to her village just two hours after giving birth.

No one here celebrates the birth of a baby; they believe that doing that could bring bad luck and early death for the child. The average family loses half of the children who are born to them. In one village where a worker from our organization went, he asked a group of women how many children they had delivered and how many had died. One woman said," I have eight living and I have lost eight." Another said, "I gave birth to six and all have died." Of the twenty or so families represented, there were none who had not lost at least one child.

When we hear stories and statistics like these, it's hard to imagine the real people and emotions behind them. I think of the precious babies I lost and how I grieved their lives; then I think of these women, living in such horrible circumstances. These women have hopes and dreams for their children just like I have. They still rejoice at the knowledge of life inside of them, hoping for a better future. These women feel their babies moving and growing inside them and dream of what they will become.

Being a mother in this culture is really the only identity and "job" for most women. When motherhood is taken away or altered, there is little hope and reason to go on. We may think that because the numbers of deaths are so great that the emotions and grief may not be; but if we are honest, we all know that this is not true. It's hard to think about the suffering and loss here especially in the shadow of my own life and the extreme excess it holds.

A few weeks ago a young woman was brought into the hospital, pregnant and unmarried. Under the traditional law of the land, she should be put to death for this "illegal" pregnancy. This week she returned saying that her baby had died, and she had miscarried. Upon examination though, it was discovered that a late-term abortion had been performed. We can only speculate what the truth was; the operation could have been forced upon the girl by her family or it could have been her own decision, knowing she would probably not be allowed to live unless she left the country. With no husband and no way to support herself, there would be little hope of survival. Either way, I'm sure she felt that she had no choice. What a horrible set of circumstances in which to make such a difficult decision.

I really can't wrap my mind around the difficult choices that are made here every day. Many of the choices these women are forced to make are not even in my scope of understanding.

It's easy to sit in judgment of people's choices when we haven't lived their lives. I am learning here that there is very little I truly understand about lack and poverty and loss of freedom and liberties. I have never really experienced any of them; the hopelessness and sadness that most here experience have never been a part of my life. I have little to offer these people. I can pray for them though, and constantly keep before me the innate beauty and sanctity of life they possess. I can ask God each day what little part I can play in relieving the pain and suffering that is such a part of life here in Afghanistan. Some days it may just be a smile or greeting that makes a woman feel that someone has noticed her and sees her as an equal.

Personal Reflection

Judging a person's choices is easy when we don't understand the circumstances in which those choices were made; even if we do, we have no idea what it is like to live another person's life. Few of us can really understand what kinds of things we would do to preserve our lives or the lives of our family members. Fear and lack can change a person; it can make people believe that they have little control over the choices they have to make. It's easy to say, "Oh I would never," but really, how can we say that? Everyone is capable of almost anything given the right set of circumstances.

The bottom line is that it is not our place to judge people; only God Himself can do that. God is the only one who understands the big picture and the condition of the hearts involved. It is my job to love and support, to love the sinner and not the sin, to show the compassion of God to a hurting and confused world.

Luke 6:37
Judge not, and you shall not be judged. Condemn not, and you shall not be condemned. Forgive, and you will be forgiven.

Letter 37 - My Weird, Wacky, Wonderful Day

Yesterday was "National Women's Day" in Afghanistan; sounds like an oxymoron to me. As a woman in Afghanistan, one has no real rights or freedoms. Women cannot choose who to marry or where to go to school or even whether to veil or not. They can never go out alone and can't drive a car; but don't worry, they will be celebrated one day each year. Actually, I wonder even how many of the women of Afghanistan even know there is holiday each year to honor them. Most don't read or write and can't afford a television.

As a foreigner, I was privy to several speeches and acts of kindness done throughout the city yesterday. I even received a rose from the children's school for being a woman. Someone said to me, "Women get this one day a year because 364 days of the year it's 'National Men's Day!' " I think that sounds about right to me.

In conjunction with "National Women's Day," I got to be a part of a special ceremony held at the Olympic Stadium. During the festivities, a skydiver jumped from a plane and landed in the middle of the grassy field, and a Black Hawk helicopter flew over and the passengers threw flyers out that rained down on the crowd like confetti. Neither made much sense to me in regards to honoring women and creating a meaningful message of appreciation; but, nonetheless, it was very exciting.

I happened to be at the Olympic Stadium because I had been asked to chaperone the school's women's basketball team to the National Finals Tournament being held at the complex. It was an honor and privilege both to be asked and to attend the event and was an experience I will not forget.

There are certain circumstances that occur in a much more expedited fashion living in a developing country. For instance, playing in the national tournament as a woman in basketball isn't very hard when one lives in an Islamic country where most women are not allowed to participate in sports and she is a part of the only school in the country with a team. There were only four teams in the tournament, one being the National Team of Afghanistan, along with the Junior National Team, our team, and a team from the university. These teams represented ALL the women in this country who play this sport. The players ranged in age from 14-24! With the unusual circumstances of this situation, it was quite exciting for our team to find ourselves a part of this tournament contending for the national title. This tournament brought out dignitaries and female members of parliament as well as generals and top male and female athletes from all over the country. In many countries, unless one is a coach of a high level team or political bigwig or celebrity, she would not even be allowed to attend such an event. Here it's a little easier. Not only does one get to attend but also she can become an instant celebrity if she is one of the only two foreign women attending along with several hundred nationals. She gets to be on the news and have film crews shoot several inches from her face for most of the day. I'm pretty sure there was more footage of my friend and me talking than there was of the game. I went from an average woman to a celebrity in this one event by just showing up!

Before you get too excited about the level of this event, I do need to rain on your parade a bit; not to diminish the accomplishments of the school's team but to bring things into perspective for you. Here is a short list of a few things that seemed a bit out of whack yesterday at this "National Level" tournament. It was a bit like Sesame Street's song, "One of These Things Just Doesn't Belong."

- *When we arrived at the state-of-the-art gym used to train Afghan Olympian athletes, it was about 40 degrees Fahrenheit INSIDE; throughout the day it warmed to about 50. I wore my gloves and coat all day.*
- *There was only one working bathroom in the gym for both men and women; and in all my travels around the world, I have experienced few worse than this one: no lock on the door, no paper, squatty in nature, and looked as though it had not been cleaned in, oh, about twenty years. I could smell the bathroom before I entered the gym!*
- *The stadium seats for observing the game were filled with about three inches of dirt.*
- *No scoreboard.*
- *The buzzer used to denote the end of the quarters was actually*

a portable alarm, probably originally used in a kitchen to sig-
nal when baked goods were done.

- The official's table was covered with a paper tablecloth — birth-
day theme — with sports balls around the edges.

- The official referee for the games was wearing jeans and a
leather jacket and COWBOY BOOTS and talked on his mo-
bile phone several times during the games.

- When we got to the final game for 1ˢᵗ and 2ⁿᵈ place, we discovered that the "cowboy" ref was also the national team's
coach.

- There were no locker rooms for the girls to change in or any
place for them to keep their things.

- The concession stand only sold items in bulk; so if people
wanted a soda, they had to buy several one liter bottles; a box
of cookies actually was a whole case!

- We were locked inside the gymnasium by armed police guards
and large metal gates.

- The top three teams received Olympic warm-up suits in sizes
X, XX, and XXX.

- The winning trophies were made of plastic and had hand-
drawn personalization plaques taped to them depicting the
event and the type of award it was.

- During one of our games, the next team to play actually
warmed up on the court while our team was at the other end
of the court making a basket.

- During one game, the ref blew the whistle and stopped the
game because a woman crossing the court with her shopping
bag was almost knocked over — she was standing in the middle
of the girls fighting for the ball.

- The girls were required to cover their heads with a chadar
while they played basketball and several of the players wore
rhinestone-studded bracelets and bling-embellished under-
shirts under their uniforms; most also had big plastic clips in
their hair.

- The team that won second place was the current Afghan

national team; they had never lost and were so mad and up-set at not winning the tournament that they would not come forward to receive their award. Instead, they sat in their seats and pouted, even though they were asked several times by the officials to come forward.

- *Quote of the Day*: While our girls' team was playing, I heard our coach ask one of the players, "Who are you guarding?" The player answered, "The girl in black." The other team was wearing black shirts, black pants, and black head wraps. The coach then asked, "Which girl in black?" The response, "The one wearing eyeliner."

At one point during the game, the ref blew the whistle for a violation of three seconds in the lane, only there was nothing painted on the court to depict the lane and the team member he had penalized had no idea what he was talking about. At another point, one of the girls ran the wrong way down the court and almost scored for the other team.

As odd as the day was, I still couldn't help but be in awe of what I was witnessing. It was absolutely thrilling to realize the implications of what was transpiring before me. In a country where women basically have no rights and few freedoms, and women's births and deaths are not even recorded, I was getting to be part of history for this country. Young women from all over Afghanistan came together to play a recreational sport, in pants and, in some cases, wearing an underscarf without the full headcover, being recognized by male officials and dignitaries on "National Women's Day." It may seem laughable and insignificant in comparison to Western culture, but it is a big step for the women of Afghanistan. Maybe someday some of these very women may have the opportunity to compete in the real Olympics representing their fellow sisters and showing off incredible achievements against so many odds. Maybe someday I will be able to say I witnessed the small beginnings of a revolution for women brought on by the participation in a sport.

What an honor it was to be a part of such a weird, wacky, wonderful day!

Personal Reflection

Being a part of this event on National Women's Day in Afghanistan was truly a once-in-a-lifetime experience. It really was remarkable, considering that less than ten years ago this country's women were not allowed to be educated and were kept like prisoners in their own homes. The freedom represented by this event was nothing short of revolutionary. I can't imagine what it must have been like for those young women to run up and down a basketball court playing a recreational sport reserved for men, wearing pants, and letting their hair flow free. Though small, it was a beginning of a new kind of freedom for these women. Even if it never progresses further, this will be something they carry in their hearts forever and may spark a desire and quest for more.

Psalms 118:24
This is the day the Lord has made; we will rejoice and be glad in it.

Letter 38 - The Joy of Being Known

As I sit down to write this week, I find things harder than usual. They shouldn't be. On the surface, things are better than they have been for a long time. We have had four days with steady electricity and minimal internet problems. The sun is shining, and the temperature each day is reaching into the 70's, a very welcome change from last week, when there was still snow on the ground and the temperature in the house was 45 degrees. I am well provided for; we are all healthy; and I have a warm bed to sleep in at night and a safe house to stay in during the day. I have enough money to go buy the food and supplies we need, and I have a wonderfully supportive family. But even with all of this, I am finding it hard to maneuver through my days. I don't know if it's the mundane routine of each day, if it's spending so much time alone, or if it's just the heaviness and grayness of this place that seems to seep into every pore of my being.

I have noticed that I am much less patient with the difficulties here right now. When at the market this week, I just wanted to scream at the men staring at me and say, "Really? What are you looking at? I'm covered from head to toe; all you can see is my nose. Is it really that interesting?" Because of all the rain, the roads are in very bad shape right now, so while traveling home from the market I was hot and carsick and everywhere I looked I saw gray dirt and masses of people. The smell of the hanging meat was stronger than usual; the way the shopkeeper talks to my husband instead of me when I ask a question annoyed me. The open sewers full of human and animal waste repulsed me and the five stops at different stores to get my grocery items exhausted me. I can honestly say these things have never really bothered me so much before, but this week I wanted to jump on a plane and go anywhere green and Western. I know I'm being selfish and prideful to think that I should have anything any different when there are so many people suffering around me. This week, even consciously knowing this, I still chose self-pity.

It's hard to battle all the feelings rolling inside of me: the feelings of guilt for having so much when others have so little, the feelings of disgust toward the backward way of doing things here, the feelings of hopelessness at all the poverty and oppression, the feelings of loneliness and insignificance with the loss of freedom and mobility, the feelings of love and friendship for the Afghans I know, the feelings of pride for the amazing accomplishments that my husband and others are having in their projects, the feelings of gratitude at how well my children have adjusted and the amazing lessons learned by us all, the feelings of honor and thankfulness at having the opportunity to live in such a place, the feelings of fear and anxiety of returning home and wondering how we will all adjust, and the feelings of grief as I prepare to say goodbye to this crazy, hard, wonderful, amazing adventure. I'm just not sure where to put all the swirling feelings. I'm not sure my heart can hold them all.

I do have an amazing outlet for some of these feelings right now, as our oldest son is visiting us. He arrived on Sunday and went to work the next day teaching at the kids' school. His younger brother and sister are almost giddy to have him around. I didn't realize, until he arrived, how very important it was to me to have one of our older children come and experience our life here. There is something very significant about "being known." Our family has never been separated before like this; I didn't realize how much it affected me that our older children had no concept of our lives and work. Having our son here to walk our journey with us, even for a few weeks, has brought some grounding to me. Knowing that at least one of our older children will have an opportunity to love and appreciate this place and its people like we do is an amazing feeling. I just wish we could share it personally with all of our children and extended family and friends.

I think one of the most important things we can do for the people of Afghanistan is represent them. Most of the people here in this country will never be able to do that for themselves. The West has a very limited view of life here, and few people have been able to see firsthand what it is like. The more foreigners who come here, the more the world is able to understand what life is really like for these people.

The people of Afghanistan need advocates: allies who will stand up for them, people who will cry out for them, who will stand in the gap for them. My prayer is that through this adventure, at least our family and our circle of friends can be just that. I realized this week, after my son got here and seeing how grounding it was to be known by him, that it was no different for this place. The world really doesn't "know" Afghanistan, and what they think they know is not a good representation of the people and culture here. The desire I have for myself and my children to understand life here is the same need that every Afghan has. The Afghan people desire to be known by the world for who they really are and by the God who created them. It is my hope that through this experience, in spite of my pride and selfishness, my world will come to know Afghanistan in a new light, in the light of Truth.

Personal Reflection

The last part of this letter is exactly why I am writing this book. As I returned from this place, I knew that God was asking me to be that spokesperson. I wrestled with all the reasons why I shouldn't and why there were many other people more qualified than I to do it; but in the end, I knew God was asking me to set aside all the questions and insecurities and simply obey Him. These pages are the result of my trying to be obedient to the Lord. For some reason He picked me to be the vessel through which these stories are told. God spent a lot of time and effort getting me to a place spiritually and physically where I could see firsthand the love that He has for the people of this nation, and I am honored and blessed with that gift. I desire to be a voice for those who have none, to represent a people who have either been overlooked or misrepresented. God has asked me to help the world see a snapshot of a place that needs the prayer and support of the body of Christ, a place that few have been and most will never have the opportunity to go. God desires the people of Afghanistan to know Him and to be reconciled with their Creator; and they need each of us in order to see that come to pass.

My prayer is that as you read the words on these pages, you are moved with compassion for the things that move God's heart, the people He has created in His image. I also pray that you will stand in the gap for them and be a voice for the voiceless. Pray for the protection of Afghanistan; pray against the evil that dominates every aspect of the society.

Pray for the leaders of the nation and pray for unity and peace; but pray mostly for the saving knowledge of Jesus Christ to permeate and illuminate every dark corner of this broken and lost nation.

I Thessalonians 5:17
Pray without ceasing.

Letter 39 - "Salaam" Afghan Hospitality

One of the biggest honors in this country for a foreigner is to be invited into an Afghan's home for a meal. Hospitality is very important to Afghans and great care and attention to detail is given in order to show hospitality to guests. Hospitality is really viewed as a religious obligation. Everyone must be ready to give "daily bread" to his neighbor. Sharing a meal together, even tea, indicates a relationship, a friendship. It is called "the right of salt" and places great responsibility on the guest to be faithful to and honest with his host. An enemy would avoid drinking even water if given from the hand of his enemy. There is a very common story told to children as they grow up in Afghanistan to help them understand the importance of hospitality.

"One night, a group of thieves entered a man's house while all of the family was asleep. The thieves, under the instructions of their leader, began carrying out carpets and cushions - anything portable that had any worth. In the dark, the leader of the band reached into a cupboard, finding a hard smooth rock-like object. He immediately decided that it must be some kind of a gem. The thieves had almost finished their work when the leader put this "gem" to his lips.

Tasting it, he was not only disappointed at finding that the gem was just a block of salt, but he was horrified that he had stolen the property of a man whose "salt" he had eaten. He immediately ordered his men to return all of the property to the house before the family awoke."

Our family was privileged to experience this honor when we were asked to share a meal with some of our Afghan friends. It was an added treat that the invitation came while our son and a dear friend were visiting. The invitation came during the celebration of Nowruz, the Afghan New Year. During this celebration, many families will have "special" guests into their homes. The Afghans will spend several days in preparation for the holiday cooking, cleaning, painting, buying new clothes, and visiting friends and family.

Our evening began upon arrival with family introductions. Only the men and children, along with the matriarch of the family, were included in the introductions. In this case, it was the mother of the sons in the household who had been a widow for many years. The sons all live in the family house along with their wives and children with "Mother." One other son lives in another home; he has six children and needed more room. The wives were not included in the introductions as they were behind the scene preparing the meal. After introductions, we removed our shoes and put on house slippers and then went into the "family" room. The family room is a general meeting room without furniture but lined around the walls with toshacks (long pillows). On the wall was a large picture of the family's late father. We were seated by family groups, the head of the family, the oldest son at the head with his mother next to him, and our family at the other end with my husband at the head of our group. After a short time of conversation, a water pitcher called an aftahbah was brought in by one of the younger sons. The aftabah, along with a large basin, went from person to person as we all washed our hands in preparation for dinner.

After we washed, the food began to arrive. A large plastic mat, called a dastarkhan or sofrah, was placed on the floor in front of us, and all the food was placed on it. At one end of the mat were dishes and glasses and silverware. The oldest son stood in the middle of the mat and passed out the serving items. Another son passed out drinks. Then the procession of food began. There was mantu, a dish of dumplings stuffed with lamb and vegetables topped with cilantro and a red sauce. There was lavash, thin Nan bread that was distributed to each person. Palau, a traditional rice dish, was presented next. There was also a dish called ashak, pasta filled with leek and mint. There were plates filled with sliced tomatoes and cucumbers as well as a large bowl of oranges.

The dishes were served by the oldest son at the Afghan end of the sofrah and by me to our foreign group. The food was delicious, and we all ate our fill. When we were finished, we left some food on our plates; if the plate is emptied, the host would continue to fill it, saying, "You are still hungry."

After dinner was eaten and the dishes removed, we enjoyed tea. The traditional green tea was served with small sweet candies and was served from the middle of the sofrah by one of the sons.

After the tea, my daughter and I were invited to go upstairs and visit with the wives and children. We don't speak the same language, so there was a lot of smiling and gesturing and saying "tashakor" (thank you) over and over.

We returned to the family room for more conversation about politics and the current situation in Afghanistan. The host's children were brought in to read and write English for us, the first generation of girls in the household to attend school where English was taught. The children are doing a wonderful job, and their father is so proud. The children's father told us, "The only way for the situation in Afghanistan to change is by educating our children, both girls and boys." He speaks four languages and yet can read or write none; he was forced to leave school at age ten to help support his family. As his daughter read English to us, he beamed with joy!

After the visiting, it was time to say our goodbyes. We changed from our house slippers and went downstairs where the family lined up to say thank you and Happy New Year.

It was a lovely evening and we all felt so honored to be in our dear friend's home and be able to share a meal with him and his family. The meal probably cost the equivalent of a week's salary for the family, but the gesture sealed a covenant of friendship that will last a lifetime.

Personal Reflection

As we shared a meal with this beautiful family, I was reminded of what a miracle it was that we had the relationship we had. It didn't make sense from the perspective of either of our cultures, our diversity a backdrop to everything. Yet here we were, families from countries that are more often seen as enemies than as friends, eating dinner together, sharing the most sacred event between friends in this culture. It was God Who brought our families together. We are knit together with a supernatural love that is bigger than any of us. There is a loyalty and trust between our families that shouldn't exist, but it does. It is beautiful, and speaks louder and more clearly than the English spoken in our home or the Dari spoken in theirs; it speaks of a God Whose plans and thoughts are higher and greater than ours could ever be. It speaks of purpose and destiny and the love of a Creator for His children, love shown through the simple joy of friendship.

Isaiah 55:9
For as the heavens are higher than the earth, so are My ways higher than your ways, and My thoughts than your thoughts.

225

CHAPTER 11 – The Beginning of the End

Revelation 21:1

Now I saw a new heaven and a new earth, for the first heaven and the first earth had passed away. Also there was no more sea.

Letter 40 – Oman—A Sweet Gift

One major perk of living in Asia is being in close proximity to so many interesting countries and cultures, countries we would never have the opportunity to visit if we weren't living in Afghanistan. This week is Spring Break for the school our children are attending, so we decided to take advantage of the time and visit one of the interesting countries so close to our home. We spent several weeks scouring the internet and asking people about all the possibilities. We finally decided on Oman.

Oman is a small country whose borders touch the United Arab Emirates (UAE) and Yemen. Oman is an oil country, Arabic in nature and predominantly Muslim. Oman is mostly desert, dry and hot except for its farthest southern tip, which is tropical because of the seasonal monsoons, and has a constant year round temperature in the high 80's. The little coastal town we decided to visit is called Salalah. Salalah is surrounded by low, rocky mountains that are gray and brown during the dry season; but in the summer, after the rains, it turns into a beautiful, lush tropical paradise. People from all over the Middle East come and spend time in Salalah to escape the extreme desert heat of summer.

We are visiting during the last part of the dry season; and though it's not as lush and green as other times of the year, it still holds its own kind of beauty. The resorts are quiet and peaceful and much cheaper than during high season. The gift of being outside and feeling the ocean breeze on my face and the golden sand under my feet is a sweet gift no matter what time of the year it is.

From Kabul, we had to fly into Sharjah in the UAE, then on to Muscat, Oman, where we spent the night and the next day enjoying our introduction to Oman. Though Oman is predominantly a Muslim country, as a foreigner I am not required to wear an abaya and hijab. I can even wear short sleeves and capris, true freedom compared to

Afghanistan. Because the country of Oman has known little conflict and war, the people are very open to visitors and are warm and friendly. Most people speak at least some English. Men wear the traditional sheik shroud and beautiful intricately embroidered scarves that they tie into turbans on their heads. Most of the Omani women are Muslim and wear the traditional black abaya with a black hijab; most cover their faces with a veil with only the eyes showing or a complete facial covering made of sheer black fabric that can be seen out of but not into. The women are very interesting to watch as they walk through the city; they look like black Darth Vader princesses gliding across the floor. All the abayas drag the ground so as to not show the women's feet, but most women wear very high heels. The combination of the two results in women who have learned to walk very gracefully and seem to glide effortlessly from one point to another. I know that by covering their women, the men hope to keep wandering eyes at home; but seeing the beautiful black princesses intrigues me and causes me to speculate and wonder what secrets the black clouds hold. I have seen very few Omani women with their faces uncovered, but the few I have seen are strikingly beautiful with chestnut brown eyes and creamy olive complexions preserved from the harsh sunshine by being covered all their lives.

One of the most interesting customs of Oman is their way of greeting each other. The general greeting of Oman is to touch noses or foreheads with each other. As children, we used to tease each other about Eskimo kissing … rubbing noses together. I don't know if Eskimos actually kiss that way or not, but seeing two people touch noses in greeting made me laugh out loud the first time I saw it, not that I thought it was funny or inappropriate, but because it brought back fond childhood memories.

Our first day in Oman we spent in the capital city of Muscat, a beautiful Mediterranean style town sitting back from the snow white beaches of the Arabian Gulf. The city of Muscat is very laid back and warm and inviting to visitors. The town is full of American style shopping and restaurants complete with McDonalds and Starbucks. During our short and busy stay in Muscat, we visited many of the landmarks of the city, including the Royal Palace and military grounds. We spent the afternoon snorkeling in the beautiful Persian Gulf waters at the Muscat Dive Center.

The next day we flew six hundred miles south to the city of Salalah. The rest of our break consisted of lots of sunshine, sand, and the sound of waves crashing against the shore.

Our kids don't really remember being to the ocean, as they were so young when we lived in Africa; so body surfing the waves, chasing crabs to their holes, and scouring the sand for sea shells were new thrills for them. They barely made it through dinner without falling asleep in their food, exhausted from being in the ocean all day. When the kids got bored with the sand and surf, there were plenty of other things to keep them busy - from tennis to squash to lawn bowling to ping pong.

Yesterday we took a drive up the coastline and then into the mountains surrounding the area. It was a wonderful adventure complete with having to stop several times while driving so the camels could cross the road. In America, we see signs telling us to be cautious of deer crossing the road. Well, here there are signs with camel crossing warnings. We tried to stop and feed them a few times, looking like ridiculous tourists; but they knew better than to take bread from a crazy-looking white woman when they had yummy hay back at their farms. But it was fun to try; the camels are enormous and highly entertaining to watch.

As I sit shaded from the sun with the cool ocean breeze blowing over me, I can't help but think of all the amazing wonders of God's world. Every inch of this beautiful planet is full of wonder and amazement. God is so creative: He made us all in His image, but unique and individual just the same. Each part of this planet has people with special features and gifts suited to helping them live in their particular place. All have unique customs and traditions as diverse as the countries in which they live. Each place we have had the privilege of visiting has brought a new awareness of God's goodness and, along with this awareness, a new gratitude that He shares it all with us. It is an honor and privilege to meet and mingle with so many of His creation, to be restored and energized by His creative beauty, and to learn and grow from the awareness that life is so much bigger than my own backyard. I am humbled by the things that I have been allowed to experience and challenged to give back as much as I have received. I am reminded to look for the "little" things that God brings across my path each and every day; and I am determined to allow His light to illuminate the darkest parts of this world, even if it's with only a smile or word of gratitude for allowing me to share in the wonders of each man's world.

Personal Reflection

Oman was very different than Afghanistan; though both are Muslim nations, the feel is very different. I wonder though, if Afghanistan had not been at war for thirty years, if they would be more alike—warm and inviting, hospitable and relaxing. Afghanistan was like this before the years of fighting began—peaceful, open, progressive. It's so perplexing to me that two places could be so close geographically and yet so very, very far apart in other ways. It was encouraging for me to see how well the Omani people lived with foreigners, eating and shopping and drinking together, living in community and relationship together. I pray that Afghanistan will be able to experience the joy of that someday.

2 Corinthians 9:15
Thanks be to God for His indescribable gift!

Letter 41 - Spring in Kabul

Spring has finally arrived here in Afghanistan. We have had several false alarms, days when our spirits would soar thinking that the cold, damp, dark, muddy days of winter were behind us, only to find ourselves pulling out the hot water bottles for our toes and gloves for our fingers yet another day. We have now had two weeks of above freezing temperatures, and the ice cream man is making his rounds again, signaling full steam ahead into the warmer, dryer days of spring.

I'm sure as I write this you are finding yourselves in days of renewal and growth all over the world. I can imagine that in my hometown the azaleas are in full bloom with bursts of bright reds, whites, and pinks bordering houses and parks. The flowering pear trees are probably bursting with green after their displays of beautiful white blossoms. On the weekends, people are out tending flower gardens, cutting back dead branches, and mowing the first growth of the green grass. Everyone seems to be in a better mood and there is hope as each day is blossoming with new growth and color.

It's the same here, only on a much smaller scale. Even in the middle of summer there is very little grass, mostly dirt and dust. However, the few remaining trees are sprouting with flowers and leaves. The almond trees are especially beautiful, blooming with beautiful delicate white flowers. The rose bushes are full of growth, stems sprouting from dead twigs that are now bushes, loaded with leaves and buds of color in just a few short weeks. I'm excited for the days to come as the roses bloom out of every corner of this dark, dusty world again - a true sign that there is always hope and that God always leaves a remnant of beauty in every desolate place, a metaphor to me that God is always present in our lives—the Creator seeking reconciliation with the creation. In every situation, no matter how dark, desolate, or dead it may appear, there are always signs of hope and beauty. The signs of spring should point us all to that hope—all things new.

It amazes me each spring how things can visually go from dead and barren to full of life. How does it happen? How can things be so harsh and ugly and appear to be dead and then, with only a little water and sunshine, burst into life? It truly is a miracle. The Bible says that as long as there is life on this planet, there will be seasons; planting and harvest, death and life, mourning and joy. It's a promise that gives us renewed hope and energy to continue, even when things seem hopeless. I think that promise is especially meaningful to me while I am in this country. There are certain things that will continue no matter what happens, no matter how bad things seem.

In the last two weeks there have been nine suicide bombings in Afghanistan; many lives have been lost in the crossfire of conflict and evil, a daily reminder that this country is at war. The days are filled with fear and sadness and destruction for the people of this nation. In spite of the tragedies, there are pockets of hope and life everywhere: men and women who work and long for better days for this country; people believing and trusting that below the hard, dry, dusty surface of soil there is life crying to break free - life full of color and beauty, life that represents the same hope and rebirth that the buds of spring hold.

I am grateful for the hope that each season of our lives brings. Change and transition are difficult, as life ebbs and flows with joy and sadness, birth and death, setbacks and growth. Life is like the seasons of a year; it's all temporary and eventually it will transition into something new. Though some seasons are better than others, and some produce more beauty and growth than others, each is dependent on the other to create a circle of growth, life, rest, death and then back again. All are parts of a whole. This represents a predictable truth that with patience, life and beauty will always burst forth from the cold and death of "winter!"

As I sit on my roof soaking in the warm sun of spring, I wish that it would last forever. However, I know that without the cold and harsh winter I would never be able to truly appreciate the joys of spring. God gives us seasons of life so we can see the good in every place we find ourselves. We have the knowledge and hope that the Creator is actively involved with His creation. Today I am thankful for the knowledge that my Creator cares about me and what my heart cares about. He cares for the people of Afghanistan more than He cares for the birds that announce the birth of spring. I am thankful for the rest I can have in Him as I step into each new season knowing that no matter what may come, there is always the hope of spring.

Personal Reflection

In the West, we have a saying about young people. We say that they are living in the "spring" of their lives. I guess it's because spring represents growth and being young during the process; but can't we live in the spring of our lives over and over, even when our bodies are old? Spring should represent any new work or season that comes after a long hard cold time. The spring I spent in Afghanistan represented so many new things for me. Some of them were new things that were bursting forth in my heart, things that God had been working on through the long hard days of "winter." It also represented new things that were bursting forth in the hearts of some Afghans we knew and also alluded to new and creative ideas for the work being done there professionally, socially, and spiritually.

Spring in Kabul is beautiful in a simpler way than other places in the world, but beautiful nevertheless. In the spring, new growth is breaking forth in the trees and flowers while there is still snow on the surrounding mountains; the days are crystal clear and the sky is a brilliant color of blue that I have rarely seen; things don't seem quite as ugly and dirty and not as sad and heavy. There is a renewed energy in the people and the projects; people are working and walking through their day with purpose.

During the first few weeks of spring, I loved standing on my rooftop terrace looking out over the city, taking in the colors and sights while the cool air still chilled me a bit. Those moments made me feel alive; they made me so acutely aware of life and growth! I liked the tangible feeling of excitement and energy! As I write these words, I can still remember the feeling; maybe it's because my heart is still living in "spring" with the new life of God that was planted during the winter of Afghanistan bursting forth in my heart.

Genesis 8:22

While the earth remains, seedtime and harvest, cold and heat, winter and summer, and day and night shall not cease.

Letter 42 - Treasures in My Heart

It is now just a few days shy of the two-week mark to head back home and life feels a little upside down. It's early morning, and the house is quiet except for the most obnoxious rooster you have ever heard. For the past few weeks, my eyes just seem to pop open at 5:00 a.m. no matter what. Some of it is Mr. "Cock-a-doodle-do" that I would throw something at if I could find him; some of it is the springtime change now that the sun comes up at 4:30 a.m. But most of it is the amazing number of details and "stuff" swirling around in my head. I knew this day would come. I knew it a year ago when we started preparation for this journey, but back then it seemed so far away. Now that it is before me, I can't seem to reconcile the bombardment of feelings and thoughts.

I'm sitting on the floor writing this, staring at the first group of suitcases packed in front of me. These suitcases hold what represents our life in this forgotten land. Nothing spectacular, just clothes and books and a few souvenirs; and yet the "life" they hold is nothing short of spectacular. The memories, the experiences, the routine, the good, the bad, the miraculous, the ordinary, all make up a journey for which it is hard to find words.

People have said to me, "I bet you can't wait to get home; nothing you will miss here, right?" Wrong! I am excited to get home and see my family and friends, and yes, I'll admit I will enjoy a few of the conveniences my home has. But there is a hole in my heart for the beautiful things I will leave behind. Some I will have a photo to remember; other things I will hide in my heart like a treasure.

What I will miss about Afghanistan:

- *Waking up to the view of snow-capped mountains all around me.*
- *Quiet mornings (minus the rooster) with a cup of coffee made from a teapot because the electricity is off.*
- *My tiny little "IKEA" house.*
- *My housemates.*
- *Eating dinner while sitting on the floor at our Afghan friend's home.*
- *Cardamom spice.*
- *The Afghan staff at the compound where we live.*
- *Smiles from our chowkidars.*
- *The morning routine of greetings and small talk with our staff as they start their day.*
- *Mantu (my favorite Afghan food).*
- *Our driver, who starts every sentence with "for example."*
- *The "identity" that my chadar and abaya give me here, which will be packed away and won't exist on the other side of the world.*
- *Lazy days off from work reading books and hanging out with my teenage kids.*
- *Making eye contact with the women on the street and sharing a connection that goes far beyond words.*

- *Our cook's French fries.*
- *The amazing people we get to work with and cross paths with each day who challenge and inspire us to be better.*
- *Sunrises and sunsets over the mountains.*
- *Chai.*
- *My bathroom that can be cleaned by hosing it down.*
- *Fresh spinach bought on the street and not in a plastic bag.*
- *Fresh fruit.*
- *"Movie Night" with our Afghanistan BFFs.*
- *"Lock down"- which really means a day off from work and school to hang out and make cookies.*
- *The smell of the spiced soap that the Afghans use to wash with before prayers.*
- *The fat bottom sheep.*
- *Kabobs with naan bread.*
- *The chatter of the children playing next door.*
- *My children having meaningful relationships with their Afghan friends.*
- *Picking out a different chadar to wear every day and not having to worry about what my hair looks like.*
- *Trips to Dubai.*
- *Hearing my husband running stairs for exercise every night when he gets home.*
- *Watching our staff greeting each other every morning as if they haven't seen each other for a year.*
- *Shopping in a grocery store where everything is like a treasure hunt and new treasures arrive weekly.*
- *Having a view for miles while hanging clothes on the clothesline that is on our roof.*
- *Lemon tea at the Korean restaurant.*
- *Chocolate croissants at the bakery.*
- *Saying "Salaam alaikum."*
- *Feeling the sun on my face, the only thing uncovered.*
- *Family style meals with a whole house of strangers who end up being our friends.*

- *Hearing at least three languages every time we go out.*
- *Rubbing shoulders and sharing vision and goals with people from all over the world.*
- *Eating hot, deep fried samosas with our driver bought from the street vendor at the local market.*
- *Hearing a world perspective in conversations instead of an "American" perspective.*
- *Hearing my husband's excitement when he comes home every day and answers my question of "How was it?" with "Crazy!" and then going into all the amazing upside-down things that happened that led to life-changing conversations about medicine and life.*
- *Not hearing my phone ring.*
- *Not having to do things because the electricity is off.*
- *"Shopping and Errand Day" with my husband.*
- *Cozy blankets and picture windows where I can watch it snow and rain.*
- *The roses.*
- *The people.*
- *The journey!*

Personal Reflection

There is not a day that goes by that I don't continue to miss the things on this list. What a faithful God I serve, in that while living in a country at war, in one of the most impoverished and suppressed nations, I can have a list like this one. One of the greatest lessons I learned while living in Afghanistan is how to live in peace - not an outward peace but an inward one. It's so ironic that God sent me to a place that is the antitheses of peace to teach me how to abide in a place of trust and comfort and peace with Him.

The things I miss the most about Afghanistan are things that I carry in my heart every day. They remind me to transfer my life lessons found in this crazy place into my home and life.

They remind me of how much God loves me and how much He desires for all of us every day.

Even today, I get such a kick out of the look on the faces of people when they ask me about Afghanistan and I tell them that I miss it every day and wish I were there again. Almost everyone is completely speechless and they stare at me, like the information doesn't quit compute. I guess it actually doesn't - how could it? It doesn't make sense, especially with what the West knows about Afghanistan. But it makes sense to me; and, hopefully, by putting these words to paper, it can make sense to others too.

Luke 2:19
But Mary kept all these things and pondered them in her heart.

CHAPTER 12 – An Unexpected Grief

Isaiah 53:3

He is despised and rejected by men, a Man of sorrows and acquainted with grief. And we hid, as it were, our faces from Him; He was despised, and we did not esteem Him.

Letter 43 - Roses in the Dust

Well, this will be my last letter from this side of the world. In just a few days we will head home and try to step back into life there. It's hard to wrap my brain around the fact that this journey is coming to a close. It seems like only yesterday that I was trying to imagine what living in Afghanistan would be like; now I am wondering how I can give it up. This journey has taken me from one end of the emotional spectrum to the other and back many times, sometimes all in the same day. This country is a land of contrasts and extremes; great joy and great sadness. In one short drive I see so many amazing things—a old man with a cart being pulled by a donkey next to a $150,000 dollar Land Rover; a man in a suit walking next to a man in a turban and traditional salwar kameez (traditional Afghan clothing); children playing in the dirt while a security guard stands by holding his machine gun; a kabob stand cooking all kinds of meat while a beggar is starving next to him. I see a billboard-sized plasma display screen above an open sewer with dead dogs and trash floating by. I see a woman wearing a burka walking down the street covering her business suit and her black eye as she walks to her office job. The assault on my senses is overwhelming, and often there is nowhere to file the pictures and the emotions as I go about my day.

As I reflect on this journey, I have to admit that though at times it has been difficult and confusing; the journey, as a whole, has been one of the most amazing and rewarding and sweet of any of which I have been blessed to be a part. Though the location and details of life are vastly different from my home country, the bottom line is that we have learned to live in this place. We go through our days doing what we can, taking care of our children, socializing with friends, being a part of activities and projects, sleeping, eating, cooking and cleaning; really not so different than life anywhere else. Yes, we have had to adjust to restrictions and dirt and guns and bombs and poverty, but life still moves forward. We have just learned to live it a bit slower and with more deliberate steps.

It was my hope that, in learning to live in this land, we would find the hidden beauty, forgotten and feared. I think we have done and seen just that. As I think of my time here, it's not the difficult things that come to mind; it's the beauty and splendor of a culture and its people, a life surrounded with grace, love, and support. It's the hidden treasures of conversations and encounters with people I have learned to love and respect which are tucked into my heart. It's the simple things of nature and provision and protection that fill my heart with such gratitude that I feel it will burst. It's the knowledge that my Creator loves me and cares about every little thing I do, think, and feel, and the reflection on the fact that the Creator loves and cares for these people, too. It's the realization that for our kids this journey will shape and alter them and their futures forever. It's the simple gifts that each day brings, filling my life with a richness I haven't known or haven't taken time to know. It's the gifts of family, relationships, time, provision, and protection that bring tears to my eyes when I reflect upon them. Mostly, it's the gift of this journey itself for which I am most grateful. My eyes have been opened to so many things physically, emotionally, and spiritually; and those things are changing the way I live and think.

In these months, as many have graciously read these letters, it has been my wish that you too would glimpse the beauty of this land and its people. I hope that I have stirred a desire for you to think beyond the borders of your life and remember a people who suffer and long for freedom and truth. Most of all, I hope that in some way I have stirred some of the same things in you that I have wrestled with so that you can find the beauty in your own journey.

*Thank you so much for traveling with me, taking this journey with us. I hope it has blessed you and given you gifts like it has me. Here's to the journey, to the gifts, to the fears, to the sadness and joy and to the wonder and amazement of...**Finding Roses in the Dust!***

Personal Reflection

As I reflect on my time in Afghanistan and remember that we did learn to live in that place, and we learned that life really wasn't so different at its core than our lives in the West, I am challenged to see the wonder and lessons and "roses" of my everyday life right here in America. My family, my friends, my "calling," and my opportunities are layered with beautiful roses that spring out of the dirt and trash of my life. The roses bring beauty and color to my season of dull, gray, and disappointing days of "winter."

I am challenged to be aware of what God wants to do in and through me every day, no matter where I live and no matter what I face.

Galatians 6:9
And let us not grow weary while doing good, for in
due season we shall reap if we do not lose heart.

Letter 44 - Six Weeks and Counting!

That's how I started my letters about this journey, and that is how I am finishing it. I am now six weeks and counting since my return to America and it has been nothing but a whirlwind of emotions, changes, and ups and downs.

During the first week of arriving back in America, we drove up north for our oldest son's college graduation and celebrated his engagement with our extended family. We moved him back home, interviewed at a new school for our two youngest children, attended two welcome home parties, visited countless friends and family, and I made my first shopping trip to Wal-Mart. Under the best of circumstances, it would have been a difficult schedule to keep up with, but I was doing it with jetlag and a heavy heart. Though at times it was tough, God graced me with everything I needed to do all that was required of me, and for that I am forever grateful!

Moving home has proven to be harder than moving to Afghanistan. The pace and expectations of American life are, at times, more than I can keep up with. Don't get me wrong, I love the convenience of America and the freedoms and availability of everything; but it all gets a little out of hand at times.

I miss my tiny little apartment and my snail-paced life. I miss having my husband home for dinner every night without a pager or an on-call schedule. I miss the simple pleasure of company stopping by for a cup of tea. I miss lazy weekend days reading books and playing games. I miss the one-day-a-week shopping date with my husband that included an uninterrupted lunch. I miss not having to juggle two practices and four appointments every day. I miss the beautiful snow-capped mountains and fiery sunsets. I even miss the obnoxious rooster that woke us every day at 4 a.m.

As I adjust to life back in the good ol' US of A, I am trying to hang on to the treasures of my last year; but it's hard. The world runs on a different time line here than in Afghanistan and, quite frankly, it makes my head spin.

There is not a day that goes by that I don't think of my home on the other side of the world. I wonder what the days are holding for my friends and colleagues. I wonder if people are safe and happy. I wonder if my Afghan friends are doing well and if they will ever think of me.

There has been a lot of recent terrorist activity in Afghanistan - bombings and killings - security is not good and many of our foreign *friends are traveling, going on holiday until things settle down. I wonder how they feel about returning to such uncertainty.*

I listen to the news with more intensity now, listening for details of my former home. To me, the women and men and soldiers of Afghanistan are not just numbers; they are real people with real lives, families trying to survive in a hostile land. I am prompted to pray for these men and women by name and for their situations, and to pray for all the others that no one sees or hears about.

In a way, the last year seems like a dream, a collection of memories that happened in a place so foreign it might as well have been the moon. Time seemed to go so fast while we were there; before we knew it, it was time to say goodbye. As we said our goodbyes, we did so with a deep sadness, feeling like we were not yet done. We knew there was so much more to do, so many more stories to tell, so much more Truth to be spoken. At the same time, we knew it was time for this part of our journey to end and another to begin. I had no choice but to trust God with the new journey and pray that He would continue to help me find "Roses in the Dust" each and every day.

Personal Reflection

The weeks and months after returning home were challenging and emotional. Though I went through the motions and somehow, with the Lord's help, accomplished all the tasks and made all the appointments in my schedule, I felt like I was in a fog, living behind a glass looking out into my life, separated from it all by a barrier. I later came to realize that the barrier was actually grief. When I left Afghanistan, it was like something inside of me was left behind; grieving the loss of the life I had, the people I left behind, and the country I had grown to love. Sometimes I felt that my heart would break for the loss; it felt like there was a huge wound in my heart. With time, the wound slowly began to heal and I had more and more days that felt like I was living instead of just surviving. I made a decision: I had to bury the life I knew and start living a new one. At first I was very rebellious to the process and felt guilty for thinking about living in my home country again. I felt guilty that I had so much while others had so little. I felt guilty that my co-workers and colleagues were still living in Afghanistan while I was home with my family and friends. The first time there was a bombing after we left, I thought about my friends and Afghan family for days, praying for them, wishing I were there in lockdown experiencing the situation with them. I didn't want to be in America; I wanted to be stuck inside our home with our housemates talking through the details of the situation together.

Slowly I was able to begin to work through the grief of leaving Afghanistan and to embrace what God has for me here. Now, instead of weeping for what I have lost, I can celebrate and embrace what I have. I can go to the beautiful memories anytime I need a Kabul "fix" and yet live in the present, concentrating on what the Lord has for me in the next season of my life. No matter what it is, I am confident that the Lord will help me continue to find the "roses." Though I am living a different life now, I will continue to stand in the gap for Afghanistan. I will continue to tell the stories and pray for them and ask others to do the same. Afghanistan will always be a part of who I am and I know my journey will always be a part of molding me into the person God is creating me to be.

2 Timothy 4:7
I have fought the good fight, I have finished
the race, I have kept the faith.

PART THREE

Lessons from the Journey

CHAPTER 13 – Seeing Through God's Lens

John 12:46

I have come as a light into the world, that whoever
believes in Me should not abide in darkness.

Afghanistan has been in darkness for centuries, its people in bondage to fear and lack. The country is financed by war and drugs, many of its leaders motivated by greed and a lust for power. One of the greatest "roses of truth" the Lord taught me during my time in Afghanistan is to love the sinner and hate the sin. At times it is extremely difficult to see past the evil, the greed, the pride, the sexual perversion, and the twisted practices of religion in Afghanistan. On many occasions, God reminded me that without Him, I am just like the people who are doing so much evil. "If not for the grace of God, there go I." Seeing the people of Afghanistan the way God sees them has helped me love them in an entirely new way.

I believe one of the reasons God gave me the gift of this journey was to help me be aware of some of the ugliness clogging the flow of grace and mercy in my own heart. We all have beliefs and prejudices that we carry through life which cloud our perspective. Is my love for my children any different from an Afghan mother's love for her children? The challenge is to look past the sinfulness and find the compassion in our hearts to stand in the gap to pray. We cannot ignore the sin or injustices done; but as followers of Jesus, we must remove our prejudices and see people as the Lord sees them. The Lord sees Afghans as they are: beautiful creations, yet lost and ignorant of His love and mercy. He sees the potential that every man and woman was born with and how they are not living in light of that potential. God's heart as a father is broken for those He created to be His children. He desires that they come running into His arms of grace and mercy.

Forgiveness Not Deserved

Recently, as I reflected on the horrific attack of 9-11, I was astounded at how my perspective had changed while living in Afghanistan. The sadness at the death of over 3,000 innocent fathers, mothers, sisters, brothers, children, and friends has not changed, and I continue to pray for comfort for the loss of loved ones for all of the families affected by the attacks.

But my perspective has changed in that I understand, to a greater degree, God's love and mercy toward *all people*. He sent His very own Son to die for *all people* from every nation, tribe and tongue. Living day after day with the greatly oppressed people of Afghanistan, rather than viewing this nation through the eyes of 9-11, helped me to see them even more through the eyes of God's love. They are precious in His sight and 9-11 does not change the fact that God is not willing that any man perish for all eternity.

As I reflect on the stories of the lives changed because of the 9-11 attacks, as I watch the video footage and relive the tragedy, the same emotions surface as if it happened yesterday; only this time, there are new emotions in the mix. Now as I relive the events of 9-11, I think about the families and friends of the men responsible for the attacks, men who also unnecessarily died on that day because of false convictions and beliefs. Dying a martyr for the jihad does not benefit those who died or those left behind. Wives, mothers, and children will not be cared for simply because their family member died a martyr. Those left behind will have to fend for themselves in a society that gives them no support or resources. Many will live out their lives in poverty with little chance to break the cycle. The men behind the attack who died did so because, as members of a religion that has no guarantee of paradise, they believed this was the one thing they could do to give themselves and their families the best chance of going to paradise. They hoped that, by killing infidels, Allah would have mercy on them and their families. Yes, they may have been motivated by hate that day, but most likely the underlying emotion was fear—fear that if they didn't go through with the suicidal plan, they would end up in hell. Unfortunately, most likely that is what did happen that day. God did notice and was grieved that His light had not entered their hearts. He grieved for the injustices and abuse they had suffered in their lives and for the purposes and potential they never reached. Most of all, He grieved that they were eternally separated from Him. If that is His perspective, should it not also be ours?

In the weeks and months following 9-11, when our nation declared and went to war against terrorism, I had no idea I would eventually come face to face with the nation in which the men and women of my country would give their lives to fight for the freedom of the Afghans from the Taliban. I never dreamed I would walk the very streets and gaze upon the very mountains where some of my friends' children lost their lives. And I never imagined God's love for a nation of people considered by many to be our enemy would consume my heart. I believe the heart of God is grieved for the lost souls of Islam. I also believe we can ask our Creator to give us His perspective. The people of Islam are destined to live eternity separated from God. If not for His amazing grace, we would all fall to the same fate.

Loving Others Through Him

Many Muslim countries, Afghanistan included, are referred to as closed countries. That means the Truth cannot be openly shared. Public meetings, open discussions, public television, multimedia—most of these channels are not available to share the Truth. Then how are these nations to be reached? They are reached by those who are willing to go and live among the people. However, the number of those who are able and willing is few. For many years, while the borders of Afghanistan were closed, many walked its border in Pakistan praying for the nation and for the revelation of Jesus in the hearts of its people. Today there are thousands seeing the Truth for the very first time. The sacrifice of prayer by precious saints, some who have literally given their lives, has paved the way. One of the most amazing elements of our faith is that we can pray for the people of Afghanistan without traveling to its borders. Prayer is not limited or bound by time or distance. We can sit in the comfort of our living rooms and pray and be instrumental in changing the hearts of the lost. We must first be willing and then we must ask God to use us by opening our eyes and hearts to the things that move His heart. A word of warning: when you begin to see people the way God sees them, as your heart enlarges with the love and compassion of God, it is difficult to ignore the pain and suffering of those in the world around you. Praying for others will make you strangely aware that this is what God made you for. God created us to love Him and love others through Him.

Sometimes it's difficult to really love others; however, as I think more of Him and less of me, only good comes out of it, both for others and for me. Thank God His grace is present every day as I set out to do His will. This journey has taught me much about how self-centered I have been and how little I have allowed God to be in control. God will go to extreme lengths to reveal His love to people. With my consent, He moved me to Afghanistan, separated me from some of my children and all of my extended family and friends. He put me in an environment that was physically and emotionally uncomfortable. He called me to a culture that stripped me of the freedoms I had known all of my life and allowed me to experience more restrictions than I have ever known. During our months in Afghanistan, I endured uncomfortable situations and formed challenging relationships. I experienced loneliness, felt incompetent, and fought feelings of unworthiness. He showed me painful things I could do nothing about and caused people to cross my path with needs I could not help. He allowed my children to go through situations from which I could not shelter them. He allowed me to be uncertain and at times miserable all because He wanted to show me how much He loves me!

I would like to think our time in Afghanistan was about helping hurting people, and it was; but it was also about a work God wanted to do in my heart. God moved me to the other side of the world to prove Himself trustworthy, to display

His goodness in a way I had never known, and to show me He is truly the God of the impossible! He wanted to teach me that His love for me had nothing to do with my performance and everything to do with His goodness. In spite of my faults, fears, ugliness, and sin, He made me to be a vessel of His love. Because of the revelation of His great love for me, I am now able to give out of that love to help others know they too are loved.

God used the people of Afghanistan to help me see innate beauty, not only in the people there, but also in myself. If I believe God loves the people of Afghanistan and wants only good and perfect things for them, and if I truly believe He would go to such great lengths to relocate our family to the other side of the world to be used to show His goodness to others, then I believe He must want the same for me.

Our time in Afghanistan is one of the greatest treasures God has given me. Not a day goes by that I don't think about the people of that nation and the time we were able to live side by side with them. I feel my heart will forever hold its people, the land, the stories, the experiences, our teammates, the simplistic routines and depth of relationships, and the revelation of God's greatness and goodness; these are the Roses in the Dust of this broken land that I have grown to love.

After our return, I shared my heart with a friend concerning our driver in Afghanistan, asking her, "How can I love someone as a brother as much as I do when I have never embraced him in a hug or spent more than three hours at a time with him? It is contrary to anything I have ever known." My connection to Mohammed represents so many things about Afghanistan, layers of emotion about truth and its revelation. It represents a spiritual connection, a connection of the heart. God has allowed me to see these precious people through His eyes and has given me a taste of the love He has for them. In the process He has given me a taste of the great depths of the love He has for me. Out of the dust of this broken and feared land have sprung the most beautiful roses my heart has ever known.

CHAPTER 14 – The Bouquet of Obedience

John 14:1-3

Let not your heart be troubled; you believe in God, believe also in Me. In My Father's house are many mansions; if it were not so, I would have told you. I go to prepare a place for you. And if I go and prepare a place for you, I will come again and receive you to Myself; that where I am, there you may be also.

The roses I found while living in Afghanistan are varied and beautiful. Some small and obscure, others so vibrant and stunning they nearly take my breath away. Some of the roses were hidden and buried under trash and discarded items, while others could be found growing strong and straight right in the middle of the hustle and bustle of life. Some of the roses were so delicate I was afraid to touch them for fear they would crumble; and others were growing strong and powerful, reaching heights well above my head. I believe it is no coincidence these beautiful flowers grow in a land of such suffering and sorrow. I believe they are kisses from God lovingly placed in the middle of fear and chaos; life blooming in a hard and unforgiving land to remind its people that no matter how challenging things may be, there is a God who loves them and has not forgotten them.

I believe the roses I enjoyed so much in Afghanistan represent the true "roses" of God's creation, people made in His image. God's creations are as varied and beautiful as those flowers. Some are weak and fragile and others strong and straight; some are hidden and some are out in the middle of life, but each one is a most significant and beautiful part of God's garden. The people of Central Asia are some of God's "roses." It may be natural to think of them as our enemy, but they are not the enemy; satan is our enemy. Although there is an element of the people that is marked and motivated by evil, this does not negate the fact that these people were created in God's image. They have been deceived by a relentless enemy who not only seeks to kill and destroy their lives but also the lives of everyone in their world. We fight not against flesh and blood, but against every evil power of darkness. Satan's aim is to completely destroy all of God's creation and to keep people in darkness. Many developing nations are in darkness and bondage because the light of Jesus has not shown or has shown dimly. It is the light of God that brings illumination and revelation; it brings creativity and prosperity; it brings health and wisdom. These are the components that make a nation strong. I know it may be argued that this does not hold true for some oil rich countries where there appears to have been progress because of their wealth. I would question, however, that although there has been progress in technology and wealth, have those nations progressed in the core values of their society? What about the freedom and liberty? Rights for women? Equality for all? And what about the core values of honesty and integrity? In these essential areas, in lands where darkness has ruled for hundreds of years, there is very little illumination or sign of change.

Religion is strong and powerful. It has controlled and dominated people for centuries. Too often it is not about a loving and forgiving God; it is about human works motivated by fear and often fueled by a prejudice and hatred for other people. Many do not follow religion out of faith and love; instead they are following out of fear of what will happen to them if they don't. And because the religion is often so integrated into the culture, most children born into an intensely religious culture have little hope of ever experiencing anything different. Even if they were presented a perspective different than they have known, few are willing to explore it for fear of what might happen to them if they do.

The Western Mindset

It can be very difficult for an outsider to understand the foundation of fear in religion. We have the freedom of choice; freedom to learn, to test, and to prove things for ourselves with little fear of harm or the consequences. In many cultures, considering or exploring any other thoughts or beliefs or faiths can result in permanent separation from family and friends, loss of jobs, income, and homes, and in some cases, death. Those who have been born into a free society have no idea what it is like to experience these kinds of sacrifices. We know of some who have made the choice to follow Jesus and are now in hiding. They face isolation and a fear that few in the Western world will ever know.

In some countries, when a person begins to believe differently and becomes a follower of Issa (Jesus) and it becomes known, his name is added to a blacklist registry. This registry may be given to government agencies and ports of entry and exit. It may also be posted in public venues. If a person who is blacklisted attempts to gather certificates for completed schooling, register for a job, or tries to travel in or out of the country, he may be discovered and, in some cases, simply disappear. Even without this official recognition, he may still face the real probability of beatings, separation from family members, loss of inheritance, and threats of death. A woman who is estranged from her family often has no way to support herself and most likely will not survive.

It must be understood that in many countries the mindset of the people is completely unlike our Western mindset. When presented with a new truth, deception and paralyzing fear greatly hinder the ability of individuals to consider this new truth. Imagine if you were presented a new way of thinking which would require leaving behind all you have ever known or believed. Few have the courage to consider new ideas. To do so could negate everything they have ever known, everything they have ever been taught. They would be forced to acknowledge that what they have believed could be false, and that all they have put their trust in might be empty. If someone is courageous enough to consider a new truth, he must face the fact that he may be alone and destitute. This is a very difficult situation.

I once heard a story of a young girl found in a house in the Appalachian Mountains where she had been kept in a closet for her entire life. This young girl of about ten had no speech and no understanding of how to live life among other people. She did not know how to use a knife or fork, had never seen a bathroom or bathtub, and had never known the feeling of human touch. She was alive and relatively healthy, but had no real understanding of normal human life. When this young girl was discovered and introduced into the "real" world, she was filled with anxiety and fear and wanted nothing more than to return to her "closet" world. It took years and years of constant love, physical touch, and socialization to bring her to a place of living anything remotely resembling a "normal" life.

I believe that often we have the misconception that the only thing a person needs is to say yes to following Jesus. But if we only facilitate the salvation process but do nothing to disciple and mature him, I believe we are committing a huge injustice. As the body of Christ, we must be willing to pray, go to the world, and share the Truth; but we must also be willing to care for, nurture, and help mature those who choose to follow Jesus. What good is it to only present the Gospel but neglect helping people to learn to live it out? Christ died for our salvation, but He also paid a huge price to create victory here on earth for us. Jesus came that we may have life and life more abundantly. Victory in Jesus comes as we learn to walk out His plans and purposes for our lives.

What If?

I asked myself many questions while living in Afghanistan, and I continued to ask them after returning home. They are difficult questions, without easy answers.

- What if we present the Truth to someone who chooses to believe but that person has no knowledge of the great plan and purpose God has for his life?
- What if someone never understands about forgiveness of past mistakes so he can have a future?
- What if someone doesn't understand that Jesus isn't

asking us to change so we can meet Him, but rather He wants us to meet Him so we can be changed?

- What if someone never understands that freedom doesn't exist in changing the past but in living in the future, where we have the power to make good decisions?
- What if someone never understands that God's character is good and merciful and that his life can be based on God's grace, not on his own works?
- What if someone never understands the power of the Spirit of God to heal, provide, and give wisdom?
- What if someone never knows the truth of the Word of God because all he has known is that the Bible is a forbidden book and that he cannot communicate with God; and even if he could communicate with God, believes that God does not want to communicate with him?
- What if someone never understands the power of giving and receiving forgiveness?
- What if someone never understands that we war against a spiritual enemy?
- What if someone never knows he has been created in the image and likeness of God, fearfully and wonderfully made, and even known by God while he was in his mother's womb?
- What if someone never knows he has access to the very power and nature of the one true God Who desires to dwell in and with him?
- What if someone never knows how to live justly and honorably with the true and just God?
- What if someone never knows that with Jesus, he now holds the power to change a generation?

We who believe are commanded to share the Truth, to go and compel the world to be reconciled to Christ. This has different meanings to each of us. For some, *"go"* means traveling to other nations; for others *"go"* means walking across the street or across the hall. For some *"go"* means entering a prayer closet and praying for others. God calls some to go physically and others to go spiritually. Do you realize you can reach out to a nation from your very own home without ever stepping foot outside your house? No matter what the specific situation, we are commanded to *go,* to *move,* to *do.* We must each pray and ask the Lord what the command to *"go"* means in our own individual lives. We have a responsibility to disciple, teach, and help mature our brothers and sisters. Jesus said in Matthew 28:19-20,

> *"Go and make disciples of all the nations, baptizing them into the name of the Father and of the Son and of the Holy Spirit. Teaching them to observe everything that I have commanded you, and behold I am with you all the days to the end." (Amplified)*

If we have given our lives to Jesus, then our lives are not our own; we have been bought with a price far greater than we can understand. We belong to Him, and have been commanded to do His good works in the earth, not our own. 1 Corinthians 7:23 states, *"You were bought with a price (purchased with a preciousness and paid for by Christ); then do not yield yourselves up to become (in your own estimation) slaves to men (but consider yourselves slaves to Christ)"*(Amplified). If we are supposed to do His good works, what are they? Mark 16:15 says, *"And He said to them, Go into all the world and preach and teach openly the good news (the Gospel) to every creature (of the whole human race)"* (Amplified).

My Prayer

God gave me and my family a very unique opportunity to live in a nation predominantly closed to Westerners. He gave us this gift for several reasons, but I believe one of the greatest was for me to learn important lessons and to share my heart and the story of our journey, so others will be compelled to pray and intercede for the people of Afghanistan and the nations of the world. The doors into these nations have been barely open to outsiders; but I sense a time is soon approaching when the door may be fully closed to all, with the exception of those who are willing to live underground and take huge risks. In the near future, there may be a time when it will be impossible to enter these nations.

Even now, with the door barely open, few have known and experienced much in these "secret places" of the world. I feel one of the reasons I was given this precious gift is because God has asked me to be an ambassador of sorts, representing these people, being a voice for those who have none. Afghanistan needs men and women who are willing to pray for them; people willing to tell the stories of injustice, persecution, and deception in order to encourage others to go.

As the doors of many countries close to outside influence, it intensifies our need to battle in the spirit realm for these nations. As believers, we have the spiritual authority to affect things in this world. When Jesus left, He sent the Holy Spirit and gave us the power and authority given to Him. Take that in for a minute. In Jesus we are, by position, above even the angels and have the authority to speak to the principalities and powers of the spirit world. In this earthly realm, God uses His body to cause change; He has given us His power and expects us to use it.

Years ago, during a time of prayer while I was walking, the Lord gave me a vision; it is actually only one of two visions I have ever had in my life. I had been convicted to pray for an American celebrity who had been in the news frequently. After several conversations with others about the lifestyle of this person, I was convicted that I should do less talking and more praying. It appeared this person desired to do good, but didn't know the Truth. And although he was immensely talented, he was deceived by false religion. While praying,

I heard myself say, "Lord, send someone across his path to reveal the truth to him." Yet, as I uttered these words, the Lord confirmed to me what I already knew in my heart. This individual was so protected and isolated from the public, that for a person with the Truth to penetrate his world would be virtually impossible.

With this realization, hopelessness started to creep into me about how to effectively pray for him. Unexpectedly, God gave me a vision. In it, there was a large room, so large I couldn't see the walls. I was standing on a platform in the middle of the room, next to a large angel-like being. As far as my eyes could see in any direction were rows and rows of soldiers. I can't describe the uniforms or the faces. I just knew they were warriors, soldiers meant for battle. In an instant, I knew that these thousands upon thousands of soldiers were waiting for orders from me. I knew I was the one carrying the authority to put things into motion. They were trained, equipped, and standing at attention waiting on ME! I was astounded. I have always known that angels surround us, working to protect and help us; but I had no idea there were so many in my sphere of influence, and I certainly didn't know that I had the authority to give them orders. In that instant, God revealed to me that all believers have this same authority; but the enemy has worked very hard to keep this knowledge from us, knowing how drastically things could change if we truly understood the power we have been given. In that moment, I knew prayer was so much more than simply asking God for protection, or wisdom, or blessing. Through prayer, battles are won and angels mobilized to do the work of the Lord.

I also realized I didn't need to feel hopeless in my prayers. As an individual, I had the power and authority to send angels to do the work where there was no man to do it. As I prayed, I saw specific angel warriors being sent to minister to and reveal Truth in response to my command. As I continued to pray, I saw row after row of these warriors leave. Thousands upon thousands of others still stood in line, and I realized they were awaiting orders as well. A soldier responds to his commanding officer; he is a "slave" to the mission, and he does what he is commanded to do. These "heavenly" soldiers were equipped and well able to fight battles and protect plans and purposes but could do nothing without my "order." I was convicted that people may not receive help and situations may not be resolved without my direction. As I continued to pray, I released these soldiers into the lives of my children, family, co-workers, friends, and fellow workers. I realized I had the authority to reach nations and tribes in places to which I may never be able to physically travel. Although the knowledge empowered me, it did not lessen my responsibility to go and do. Rather, it expanded my influence and ability to change things through prayer.

I would like to say the vision I had on that walking path years ago kept me anchored in a place of great spiritual strength and awareness where I remain daily, but it didn't. I often forget about the authority given to me and find myself worrying and fretting about situations and people I love. Humans are like that; we have very short memories. But the Lord is good and reminds me often, through the Holy Spirit, that He is my source of strength.

You may never step foot outside the country of your birth, but you can still affect nations! You can still send the Truth to the uttermost parts of the earth. God's heart desire is for the nations of the world to know Him. Our desires should line up with His. Isaiah 6:8-11 says, *"I heard the voice of the Lord, saying, Whom shall I send? And who will go for Us? Then said I, Here am I, send me."*

It is my hope and prayer that you will allow your heart to be broken for the lost and dying of the world. I pray you will be "bothered" and "heartsick" for the injustices in the world, angered by the evil running rampant. I pray you will not simply say to yourself, "Thank God I live in freedom," but rather, "Dear God, what can I do for these precious ones in bondage?" If you are a follower of Jesus, you have the spiritual authority to stand in the gap for the helpless and tormented. Take the authority you have been given and use it to pray for the world! Send others or go yourself. We are all called to this work. Remember that you could have been one of those born into a closed place, locked inside a home with no rights or comforts. It could be your child taken to a terrorist training camp, brainwashed to kill and hate. It could be you and your family living in poverty and addiction. Pray against the evil and darkness keeping these precious people in bondage as if they were your own family. They can become your brothers and sisters in Him. See them in faith and love them as if they are already part of the family of God.

A Perfect Plan

I knew the Lord had specific plans and purposes for the people we would encounter during our time in Afghanistan, but I never gave much thought to what He had in mind for me personally. God desires that we be His vessels of love toward others, but He also desires that we gain greater understanding of His love for us. Often, the Lord went to great lengths to show me something beautiful by simply showing me His heart. God's heart is full of compassion and mercy towards people, and He desires each of us to know and experience that same compassion and mercy. God desires for us to extend His love toward others; but to do so, we must have a growing revelation of His love for us.

While living in Afghanistan, I usually had no problem walking in forgiveness with the Afghans; but at times I struggled with forgiving myself. Satan strives to keep us in bondage by focusing on our own failures, dealing with feelings of guilt and condemnation. He wants us to believe we never quite make the mark, that we are never quite good enough.

These feelings keep us separated from the heart of God and keep us from living in freedom. When we are struggling with feelings of guilt or are having trouble with rejection or self-confidence, it is very easy to operate out of pride. Pride is simply being self-focused—self-absorbed. We can be focused on our own gifts and abilities or focused on our faults and mistakes. Both are wrong. Our focus must be on the Lord. By staying focused on ourselves, we are rendered ineffective in helping others.

At times I have mistakenly believed that by admitting what I cannot do and focusing on what I have not accomplished, I am being humble. But humility is not self-condemnation; it is recognizing that any good gifts, talents, and purposes that we may possess have their origins in God. The world does not need to see weak and depressed believers. They need to see that *"we can do all things through Christ who strengthens us!"* We can overcome, be whole, and walk out the plan of God in our lives with joy and victory, all because of Jesus! God does not expect us to be perfect; He simply asks us to give all that we are to Him and allow Him to be our ability and strength.

My time in Afghanistan allowed me the opportunity to begin opening my heart to God in a way I had not previously done. Out of necessity, it allowed me to walk in His strength and grace, not my own. He covered my fears with hope, my weakness with His ability, and softened my hard heart with His compassion and love. Through this journey, God helped me find the sweet, unexpected beauty of the rugged wasteland of Afghanistan, as well as in my own heart.

After leaving Afghanistan, I began to realize how much the Lord wanted to show me every day that no matter where I laid my head at night, regardless of how hopeless and difficult my surroundings may seem, there are always beautiful roses waiting to push through the dirt of my life. God desires to feed, cultivate, and weed the garden of my heart so that the most beautiful and vibrantly colored flowers can bloom and turn their faces toward the "Son!" The pace and relentless busyness of my world does not lend itself well to finding the secret things of God. For me, it took being removed from the schedules, friends, family, and "stuff" to allow me to see the beauty and simplicity that can be found in life.

God desires for you to understand and experience His authentic love for you. He wants you to know He made you the way you are for His specific purposes, for good and not for evil. God made you to be His crowning glory, His pearl of great price, the apple of His eye, and one for whom He sent Jesus. He wants you to know His peace and joy. He wants you to understand there is nothing you can do or say to make Him love you more or less. He loves you just because He is God and just because you are! God doesn't want us to stop with simply knowing these truths; He wants us to take the next step and live it out by sharing His love with others. I am not referring only to the people of Afghanistan, but to all in our sphere of influence. Our neighbors, our coworkers, our children's teachers, the person standing in line behind us at the store - anyone.

Through this experience, I am learning that God wants to teach me how to cultivate the garden of my own heart. He wants to help me learn to prune and fertilize, turn the soil, water and weed, so that the "flowers ' in my garden can mature to be all that God desired them to be when He planted them there; He wants me to help others do the same. Whether it is the Hindu in India searching for answers, the Muslim in Afghanistan searching for grace, the Buddhist in China searching for peace, or the agnostic in America searching for significance, I believe we are all searching for God and looking to fill the hole in our souls that can only be filled with Him and His Truth. The Master Gardener is searching for workers willing to turn the soil of people's lives and plant the seeds of His goodness wherever they find themselves. He desires to help us mature and nurture the roses of life: roses that let off the fragrance of God and, through their beauty, remind us all of the God Who loves and cares for His creation.

Go ahead, start looking. Where will you find your "Roses in the Dust?"

John 3:16

For God so loved the world that He gave His only begotten Son, that whoever believes in Him should not perish but have everlasting life.

CPSIA information can be obtained
at www.ICGtesting.com
Printed in the USA
FFOW03n0701240317
33794FF